Rules of the Game

Women in the Masculine Industries

Teagan Dowler

To all the women who came before
and to those who will come after;
thank you.

Contents

About the Author

Teagan Dowler is the founder of The Blue Collared Woman; which supports individuals, associations and organisations to develop and deliver initiatives to achieve greater diversity and inclusion (D&I) within the engineering, resource and construction industries.

Teagan has significant large scale Civil Construction, Iron Ore, Coal and engineering industry experience in the areas of Human Resource, Learning and Development and Human Behaviour Coaching and Psychology. She holds a Masters of Human Resource Management and a Bachelor of Science (Psychology) from The University of Melbourne. Her career has seen her work with some of Australia's largest resource, construction and energy companies, Universities and Industry Associations.

Teagan is a leader in the area of diversity, inclusion and leadership and is regularly asked to comment on industry developments. Teagan has been quoted in The Australian House of Representatives, featured in a range of magazines (including OK! Magazine, The Collective and CLEO) and interviewed on live breakfast radio for 4BC Brisbane and ABC Gippsland. She is also a founding management committee member of the Diversity Practitioners Association in Australia.

In 2014, The Blue Collared Woman was awarded Top Instagram Accounts to Follow by Mining Global along with a finalist nomination in the Women in Industry Social Leader 2015 Awards and WIMARQ Gender Diversity Champion 2017.

To connect with Teagan please visit:

Website:
www.thebcw.com.au

Instagram:
@thebcw

Facebook:
www.facebook.com.au/TheBCW

Twitter
@thebluecw

Introduction

I thought about writing a book that would inspire people to recognise the valuable contribution women make to all industries and all workplaces. It was going to be politically correct, showcasing the skills and contributions of females and would paint a glossy picture of how men and women can work harmoniously together. I was going to discuss the multitude of data which clearly shows how diversity leads to better decision making, greater innovation and increased profits. I was going to use harmonious language and I certainly wasn't going to swear.

But then I thought, stuff that.

What we really need is a book that discusses the realities, in all their humour, awkwardness and frustration, of what it's like to be a female working in a traditionally masculine world. The worlds I am talking about are the classically masculine industries of Resources, Construction, Manufacturing and Engineering.

For centuries now, these industries have traditionally been the domain of men. If you had a vagina, please don't bother applying. In some places this was an unspoken rule, in others, such as underground mining, it was a hard and fast policy. But over the last couple of decades we've started to see more and more women trickling into these industries. Attracted by the challenging work, interesting projects, diverse locations and of course, the big dollars. Women began pursuing qualifications which gave them some access to these worlds.

With the right qualifications and the assistance of the mining boom women's opportunities began to expand. Large mining companies were hungry for human resources and began casting their nets further than the traditional recruitment pools of fathers, sons, brothers, uncles and old workmates.

Whilst there were a few women who worked in these industries prior to the boom (and they are freaking awesome if you ask me), they were scarce. These women rose through the ranks of organisations when Equal Opportunity for Women in the Workplace didn't even exist. They had to work with individuals who thought the only place for a woman was at home, cooking dinners and raising babies. They had to step onto sites and command respect from a workforce who were not used to working with women. The challenges these women faced were much more overt than they are today.

Yet whilst many of these factors appear to have lessened, the sad fact remains, women must still overcome gender-specific challenges when working in masculine environments. Whilst the pornography posters are no longer in every shed, they are certainly still in some. Some men still think it's bad luck for women to work in underground mines, there are still porno magazines on the crib shed tables, business meetings at strip clubs still take place, and yes, there are still men who think women are only suited to housework and childrearing. So whilst we appear to have changed a little, the culture of the old world still hangs around.

Clearly, the genders have not reached parity. At the time of writing the latest statistics show that 14% of mine workers and 11% of construction workers are women, whilst approximately 25% of workers in manufacturing and transport/postal/warehousing are women (as outlined by the WGEA data explorer). The pay gap in Australia currently sits at 17.9% and has hovered between 15% - 19% for the past two decades. Another important gender metric to watch is the World Economic Forum Global Gender Gap. In 2014 the World Economic Forum Global Gender Gap Report ranked Australia at 24th position (out of 142 countries) across economic, political, education and health-based criteria. Australia

2

has shown an increase in our percentage scores across the four areas, but our overall ranking amongst the other countries is slipping. This means whilst we are making small gains in eliminating the gender gap, we are doing it at a slower pace compared to other countries who are achieving better gender parity.

The question begs to be asked, why does Australia still have such poor gender equality statistics when we have Sex Discrimination Acts, Human Rights Acts, Equal Opportunity Acts, Diversity Policies, Affirmative Action Programs, corporate programs, award ceremonies, Human Resource and diversity teams? Why have we still not cracked the elusive holy grail of gender equality?

I believe it comes down to social and cultural resistance. As a society, we have focused on creating systems and legislation to address gender inequality, which is undeniably important, but we have not spent sufficient time discussing and questioning our social values, organisational cultures and individual behaviours which support or detract from gender equality. I believe this is a serious oversight for if we want to change something for our future, we need to be aware of where we are standing in our present. We need to have a good look at our current selves.

This book is designed to address exactly this: It is designed to build awareness.

Awareness of our nation's culture, the culture of our industries and the behaviours and experiences of people within these industries. Most specifically I want us to discuss the realities of what it's like to be a woman working in a masculine workplace. With the latest buzz around encouraging more women into the masculine industries of Australia I think it is important we have a good look at our current situation to

3

develop the best steps forward with our diversity and inclusion strategies because frankly, I don't think we're doing a good enough job of it.

Through this book, I wish to throw back the veils which have been carefully placed across the concept of gender equality in the workplace. These veils of political correctness have prevented us from having any real conversations between men and women about what it actually means to be a female in an environment where the majority of people are men. When the gender conversation is brought up people immediately go on the defensive; men don't want to appear discriminatory or offensive, women don't want to appear like whinging feminists. So we're left with many things unsaid and many problems unresolved. Conversations go underground as people whisper amongst trusted allies their true feelings about gender equality.

Yet, if we are ever to change the status of gender equality in Australia, this pussy-footing needs to stop. We need to tell the truth about what it's like to be a female on a mine site, a construction project, a workshop, or any other place where being female places you in the significant minority. I want women to know that it's normal for it to feel weird, uncomfortable, exciting, joyous and intimidating at times. Sometimes it's normal to experience all of those things on the same day! Most importantly I want women to have skills in their toolkit to work through the rollercoaster of experiences, to build effective work relationships and to deliver great performance for themselves and their industry.

It is through this book that I hope to:

- Be honest about the cultures that currently exist in many masculine industries to help prepare women for what they may encounter upon entering these industries;

- Open the eyes of organisations to the realities of being a woman in a "man's world" so they can understand and work towards eliminating the gender-specific challenges women may face in these workplaces;

- Help our male colleagues become more aware of their own behaviours and provide insight into the potential experiences of their female colleagues, and finally;

- Provide women with suggestions, advice and stories to help them overcome the challenges of being a minority female in the workplace.

I have chosen to use the term 'masculine industries' as a way to describe the industries which have an overwhelming majority of male employees and whose cultures espouse masculine characteristics. These types of industries are also often called the 'heavy industries' or 'male-dominated'. I use the term masculine industries deliberately throughout this book as a way to draw attention to the cultures that tend to exist in these workplaces. Cultures that include elements of assertiveness, aggression, competition and dominance, but we will go into this further later on.

What I will present in this book is an honest account of my perspective and experiences of what it's like to be a woman working in the masculine industries. To balance this approach I have presented real-life stories from over 50 other people who work in the masculine industries. Their perspectives, opinions and advice are provided to counter any of my own biases which I may have. Through this process, it has been interesting to see the same themes emerge for women across different ages, roles and workplaces. What I have found is that whilst the words of their songs are different, the tune it is sung to tends to be the same.

The stories shared within the book are the real-life experiences of women currently working in or who have recently worked in the masculine industries of Australia. It explores their own trials and errors, mistakes, embarrassment and sometimes emotionally damaging experiences. These are hard learned lessons from women who have been there and done that. It is important we share these stories honestly and provide advice with hindsight to help others avoid making the same mistakes which we have done before.

Whilst this book has been written from the experiences of people who work in the mining, resources, construction, manufacturing and engineering industries the observations and experiences are relatable to anyone who works in an environment where masculinity is the favoured characteristic. This could include other industries such as Information Technology, Finance, Science, etc. or even smaller environments such as individual companies, clubs and associations which have an overwhelming majority of male leaders and members.

When reading through this book you will notice I have kept the names anonymous of the people who have been interviewed and contributed to this book. The reason for this is to encourage complete honesty and uncensored responses to my interview questions. I've found that people are very cautious about who they share their gender challenges with and are reluctant to openly share their experiences within the masculine industries. For some women the reluctance comes from not wanting to appear weak or as though we cannot cope in an industry we've been trying to gain acceptance in. For men, the reluctance stems from a concern about saying the "wrong thing" and causing offense, which may get them into trouble.

It is with this understanding in mind that I would like to sincerely thank everyone who has bravely opened up to tell me their stories and their experiences. Thank you to the women and men who met me for a secret coffee chat, tucked away in some obscure café so their colleagues wouldn't see them, to those who completed the anonymous online survey in their own time and for my dear friends who put up with my phone calls, email questions and Facebook posts.

Thank you to the women who have let me share their stories, experiences and advice within these pages. You are an inspiration to me and others, even if at times you don't feel like it. Remember each and every one of you is a pioneer for future women entering the Australian masculine industries. Each of you inspires me to realise there are no limitations to what we can achieve, but that we might have to work hard to get there.

To all of the men who have shown respect and supported me throughout my career to date, and particularly those who encouraged me to write this book, I want to thank you; you are true gentlemen. To those of you who let me inside the world of "secret men's business", I say a massive thank you! Your insight into male dynamics not only enabled me to adjust my behaviour and see individuals and situations from a different perspective but gave me much amusement and chuckles along the way. More seriously though, it enabled me to adjust my behaviour and see individuals and situations from a different perspective. You guys are great and I can't thank you enough.

Finally, thank you, dear reader, for picking up this book. It has been a labour of love and a dream finally realised after years of hard work, late nights and weekends at the desk. Thank you for being curious, and I hope passionate, about gender equality not only in our workplaces but in our broader society. You play an integral role in shaping the future through your thoughts, words and actions, no matter how big or seemingly small they may be. Please don't ever feel as though you can't create change - because you can. Don't think that because there are more famous or more powerful people talking about gender equality that your voice is unnecessary. All too often, when we stand in the shadows of

7

giants, we forget that we are giants too. Be the giant in your own world, stand up for what is right, fair and equal, voice your opinion and challenge the status quo. Don't feel alone, we are right beside you.

My Story

I've always been a little different. Right from the word go I tended to think and do things that other kids didn't. I mean, what three-year-old doesn't want to go down a slide because they are considering all the "consequences"? The answer: Me. I was a very cautious kid, I didn't like change and I constantly needed to be kept abreast of what was happening. I was the only one in my grade who knew the direct phone number for the local police and fire brigade and I always had a back-up plan in case of emergencies (which at the age of eight pretty much consisted of not getting picked up from school or my parents dying). I guess this aversion to risk put me in good stead for a career in the industries heavily regulated by process, procedure and legislation.

However, it wasn't my first career choice to go play on construction sites or in big dirty mine sites. Rather, I wanted to be a ballerina. At four years of age, I would twirl around the lounge room with my teddy bears and dolls lined up as an audience. I liked "spinning dresses" that would flare outwards when I spun on the spot. I could play all day without getting dirt on my school uniform and eat sticky chicken wings without making a mess. I was, as my then hairdresser put it, a "real little lady".

However, all of this began to change once I began school. By grade one I was becoming more assertive and competitive. I remember sitting cross-legged on the mat answering the teacher's maths questions. I was sitting next to a boy, who I had a crush on mind you, and he was answering all the questions. I remember at that moment wanting to beat him to the answers. Yes, I thought he was cute, but I also wanted to outshine him. This desire to compete with boys inevitably spilled over into gym class. Even at a young age, I noticed how most of the boys strutted around like they were Michael Jordan or Shaquille O'Neil (basketball was big when I was young) whilst the girls sat on the sidelines. I didn't like this one bit. I believed girls had just as much potential as boys and vice versa. However, this competitive spirit was not always rewarded. At age 8, I was hauled into the Principal's office because I had been winning at four-square and kept beating two of my male friends. I remember the boys complaining my serve was too fast and that I was aiming for the corners rather than hitting it directly back to them (duh, isn't that the point of four-square). I thought they were embarrassed for being flogged by a girl and were just being sore losers. I didn't give their complaints much thought and I certainly wasn't about to ease up on them - suck it up boys, I am the four-square champion of the world! I finished recess feeling confident and cocky. However less than 5 minutes back into the classroom my winner's high was soon crushed as I found myself being hauled into the Principal's office. Apparently, the boys had complained to the teacher and said I was being mean (because I was beating them). I was devastated and shocked. I'd never been to the Principal's office before, never been in trouble and had never been called mean. I was, in general, a pretty kind kid. Yet, here I was, being told I was mean and that I was now forbidden from playing four-square. All because I was competitive and two boys couldn't handle being beaten by a girl.

In hindsight, it's an interesting message to be given as a little girl. You're upsetting the boys, you must stop. You are better than the boys, you must stop. The boys think you're mean, stop. You are too competitive, stop. Part of me wonders how this experience, which has stuck in my mind after all these years, shaped my development. I can definitely say that as the years went on I grew in my desire to beat the boys. I worked hard to be one of the top kids in class and on the sporting field and tried to show how capable girls were at any chance I got.

Of course, this was not always well received. Especially in a small country town where fitting in was key to social survival and breaking the mold was met with whispers, teasing and social isolation. All of which pretty much sums up my early teenage years. I spent the early part of high school as the girl that other kids picked on and found myself floating from one social group to the next trying to fit in. However, in a year level of only 60 kids, the social group options were fairly limited. I found myself divvying up my time between the boys who were into computers and hack-e-sack, hanging out with the kids in the year below me who I played sport with or killing time in the toilets or library.

On reflection, think I tried to suppress and forget about those times, but looking back now that experience was awful. I remember coming home from school many times in tears or depressed. It affected me so badly that I developed an eating disorder that was rooted in a need for control and a feeling that I should punish myself for not being good enough. This behaviour was with me for the majority of my high school years, until I became very ill in my final year of school. The realisation that this illness could destroy my chance of getting a good VCE score and ruin the chance of getting out of my small town, was enough to shock me out of my unbalanced behaviour. Interestingly, in the same year that I reached this realisation, three of the girls who had been part of the bullying group apologised for their behaviour towards me. A few years later, one of the boys who had been part of a group that had teased me also apologised for what he and his friends had done. I remember the discussion with the boy quite vividly as I hadn't expected him to remember what he'd been like in early high school. His apology came when we were in our mid-twenties and working on the same construction job. We had met up to grab dinner together and were chatting about life since school. Out of the blue he suddenly said to me, "Teags, we were pricks to you in high school. I'm really sorry for that". His apology was touching, but at the same time, I bore no ill feelings towards him, his friends or the girls who had been awful to me. Instead, I said to him "Yeah, you guys were shit, but to be honest, you taught me on how to deal with the same crap I'm dealing with on this site. So in essence, you trained me". He looked shocked and amused and asked what I meant by that comment. I explained that in my early years I learnt how to project confidence even if I didn't feel it. I worked hard on developing self-acceptance when I was different to everyone else. I became focused on what I wanted to achieve, even when I was made to feel not good enough. I stayed true to my competitive self and my desire to be as good as I could possibly be.

I finished school with final marks that got me into a Bachelor of Science at The University of Melbourne where I majored in Psychology. Whilst I loved psychology (and still do) it was my first-year lecturer who gave me some very influential advice - "Don't become a doctor in psychology unless you really, really want it". It was this statement that helped me realise that I didn't actually want to be a young twenty-something-year-old psychologist who would be dealing with the darker side of human nature. At the time when I was studying psychology, it seemed (to me) to be all about the psychosis and pathologies, rather than the newer perspective of positive psychology. I didn't want to be young, inexperienced and dealing with the darker side of human nature because frankly, I didn't think I would have the ability to keep my private life separate to the experiences in my work life. Nonetheless, I still consider that returning to psychology and completing my doctorate would be something I'd like to do later in life.

Once I realised this, I then had to decide what to do with my education. I still loved understanding people but my attention shifted from the psychological illnesses to understanding the nature of people in the workplace. Looking at how to get the best out of people, how to change cultures and improve organisational productivity through human factors became my interest. I decided to continue my education with a Master's of Human Resource Management whilst simultaneously working for a consulting firm with clients in the resource and construction industries. During this time I also completed a couple of stints of vacation work on different mine sites and thoroughly enjoyed the straight talking, no-frills culture of those workplaces.

On completion of this degree I had a quick stint in financial services, but missed the fast pace, grubbiness of the heavy industries. I jumped back into the construction industry on a highly controversial, billion dollar project where I worked in the Human Resources

12

department and led the Learning and Development team. From there I was able to combine my passion for psychology and organisational strategy by becoming a consultant and leadership coach primarily in the masculine industries. Through my different roles, I've had the privilege to work in civil construction, underground and open-cut coal mining, open-cut iron ore mining and steel processing. I have worked with hundreds of Managers, Superintendents, Supervisors and other business leaders to assist them in developing their people and team strategies and implement practical initiatives to translate strategy into real world outcomes. Unsurprisingly the majority of people who occupy these roles are men. This means I spend most of my time working with men: communicating, negotiating, navigating conflict and influencing their behaviour. My work often takes me to remote locations on FIFO arrangements so not only do I work with men, but I live and socialise with them as well. It's lucky that I love hanging out with blokes! On average, to work in these environments has been great. I count my blessings to have had these opportunities, but they have certainly presented different challenges.

From sites with punch-ups and death threats, sexual intimidation and harassment, denigration and dismissiveness, I've experienced the lot. These experiences made me feel personally incapable, like an outsider, whose ideas were different to the norm. After only a few years into my career, I had begun to question whether I was cut out for these industries and workplaces. My self-esteem was once again dipping and my personal relationships were suffering. I also noticed other women were dealing with the same or similar types of challenges.

It became apparent that whilst there was a handful of us (i.e. women) in these industries, the majority of roles we occupied and the influence we had on decisions was very different compared to the men. We tended to be clustered in the supporting roles, not decision-making roles and the generalised attitude towards women was not one of equality. It was very clear through the behaviours and cultural norms that this was a man's world, where men made the decisions, men solved the problems and men did the tough stuff. It was no place for a lady.

As you can imagine, these experiences awakened the competitive little 8-year-old within me. It was not right that talented women, who were smarter than men, and who wanted to make a change, were unable too because they were being kept out by a culture. I began to ask other women whether they'd noticed the same things, as I thought maybe my view was biased and completely divorced from the reality. Yet, the vast majority of women I spoke too felt the same way. They began to share stories of the challenges they'd experienced, the isolation they felt and their wish for things to change.

It was through these experiences and conversations with other women that I realised something was not necessarily wrong with myself or the other women, but that the culture of our industry was sick and completely unbalanced. This realisation and the desire to enable and encourage more diversity and inclusion in the masculine industries is what led me to establish The Blue Collared Woman (The BCW). I felt that if the small group of women who worked around me felt the same way, surely there were other women around Australia (and maybe even the entire world) who felt similarly.

Therefore, The BCW was formed with the intention to support and empower women to be confident and influential contributors in the masculine industries. We achieve this by sharing our stories across social media, supporting organisations to set diversity strategies and programs, running leadership and self-development workshops, networking events and coaching services for individuals. It has been a beautiful ride since launching The BCW and I am thankful for the opportunities to have spoken at industry events, provide professional emcee services for organisations such as NAWIC Victoria, AIPM and Engineers Australia, to be featured in a range of magazines (including OK! Magazine, The Collective and CLEO) and interviewed on live breakfast radio for 4BC Brisbane. It has given me the opportunity to speak to thousands of people about gender diversity in the masculine industries and challenge the perceptions and biases that are held around this subject.

I hope that whilst reading this book you can be as open and honest with yourself as I aim to be in my recounts and which the 50 other female and male contributors have been in sharing their opinions and experiences. The movement of diversity and equality is not about blame. It is not necessarily any person or groups fault for where we are at this current time. What we all must do however is own the responsibility of where we want to go in the future. What kind of world do we want to create for the next generation, and the one after that, and then that? I personally want to see a world where no one is restricted from following their dreams because they are different, or prevented from marrying the person who they love, or feel constrained by social or religious expectations. I want all people to be able to contribute freely and to be respected for the difference and uniqueness they offer. If we don't achieve this acceptance, we are

15

limiting the human experience and we are limiting our future possibilities. Now more than ever, we humans need a different way of working, living and thinking. To do this we must accept our past, recognise our present and make a choice about our future. The question therefore stands… what choice will you make about the future you will create?

PART 1

Setting the Scene

"A gender-equal society would be one where the word 'gender' does not exist: where everyone can be themselves."

Gloria Steinem

Understanding Gender

"We've begun to raise daughters more like sons... but few have the courage to raise our sons more like our daughters." – Gloria Steinem

Before we enter into any conversations about the behaviours of women and men in the masculine industries it is important to first establish a clear definition and understanding of what gender is.

Imagine a world where gender didn't even exist. A society where there is no need to use words like man or woman, girl or boy, his or hers. Because frankly, it makes no difference. Everyone is treated the same, everyone is equal and everyone is free to act and behave in ways that are comfortable for them.

In this imaginary society, the first question we ask of mothers with new-born babies is not "is it a boy or a girl", but rather "are they healthy"? Nor do we race out and buy frilly pink dresses or shirts with trucks on them just because the child has genitalia arranged in a certain way. We don't hug those with vaginas more than we do those with penises. Or use more words with the former and less to the later (as a side note, this is exactly what we do in our current western society). We don't feel the need to separate children into different schools. Or encourage some of them to pursue science and maths whilst others are influenced towards health and social professions. If a boy and a girl did end up in the same job we certainly wouldn't pay one of them more than the other, because after all, what impact does an appendage – or lack of one – have on someone's worth. Or their intelligence? Or their commitment to a job? We would understand that whilst some members of the community are the ones who grow little humans inside of them, the other people are just as important in getting that new life to grow. Both have equal value, just different roles. And of course, when that new person does pop into the world there is no "primary caregiver" because everyone is a "caregiver". Of course, we certainly wouldn't judge one of the "grower" individuals if they decided not to grow a human inside of them. That's totally cool too, everyone has choice. In this society, where individuals have the freedom and flexibility to be themselves, there is little difference between the number of vagina and penis owners in leadership positions and governments are made up of people who reflect the community they serve.

However, this make-believe world is so far removed from our current reality, it's not even funny! Our current society is built in such a way that gender is used to classify us, to control us and to dictate the "should" and "should-not" of our behaviours. All because of what's happening between our legs.

When a child is born, a simple glance at the genitalia is the most common determinant of what sex will be entered onto their birth certificate. Whilst this process must make the administration part a breeze, I'm going to challenge the medical community (I've always been pretty opinionated) by suggesting this is probably a bit lazy. Let me explain why…

When a baby is growing in utero its first few weeks cruise by without any differentiating sex organs. At about the 6-week mark the genes switch on and if the child has an XY chromosomal combination testes will start to develop. If it has a genetic XX combination, ovaries will develop instead. Not long after the development of sexualised genitalia, the testes of the XY child will start to produce testosterone. If the XY child (a.k.a. a male), does not receive enough testosterone at this stage he will be born with feminised genitalia. Conversely, if an XX child (a.k.a a female) receives abnormally high levels of testosterone at this early stage she will develop masculinised genitalia. In some cases, a child may be a certain genetic arrangement, but have the genitalia of the opposite gender (i.e. a genetic female with male genitalia). It can even lead to children being classified as the "wrong" gender only to discover later in life when puberty begins or when they are having complications conceiving that in actual fact, they are not the sex they thought they were. It becomes even more unclear when a child is born with a chromosomal combination of XXY, known as Klinefelter (which affects roughly 1 in 1,000 births) or when they are born with female genitals as well as testes, known as Androgen Insensitive Syndrome (which affects roughly 1 in 13,000 births).

As you see, gender is a little more complex than simply having a penis or a vagina. Yet this is how we split our society. Once the doctor declares whether we are male or female, society immediately knows how to interact with us.

The theory of gender being predetermined in the womb relies on the concept of specific male hormones (namely testosterone) interacting with the developing foetus and creating body (i.e. penis and testes) and brain circuits that are boy specific. As one author put it, the testosterone "marinating" the boy brain causes some "brain circuits (to) grow and to make others wither and die" (Brizendine, 2010). This allegedly leaves the boy child with boy-behaviour and boy-preferences: reduced interest in looking at faces and making eye contact, better motor skills, a penchant for rough-and-tumble play, a desire to take risks and break rules, to be more competitive and to enjoy moving mechanical objects. All of these things fit beautifully with the stereotypical male behaviour of being physical, systematic, impulsive and unemotional.

However, here comes the kicker. Some of the studies which gave rise to these concepts about boys have had their methods, accuracy and objectivity questioned. This means that potentially the research which we've based many of our social structures on, might not actually be legit. That it's all make-believe.

Whilst the scientists haven't reached a definitive answer to the nature vs. nurture gender debate, it is important for us to understand and consider that current scientific understanding about gender may not actually reflect the truth (GASP! Shock horror). Whilst some researchers find evidence to support gender differences, others have questioned how accurately these studies were conducted and even whether the researchers were free from their own gender perceptions and biases. In some cases, other studies have found absolutely no sex differences in supposedly male behaviour between young babies. Cordelia Fine, the author of Delusions of Gender does an excellent job of blowing your mind with these types of studies, making you question everything you thought you knew about gender.

So where does that leave us when even the scientists can't agree on how gender is established. Some say it's purely genetic and our behaviour, preferences and thoughts are completely at the mercy of our genetic arrangement. Others say gender is the fabrication of a society that needs to classify, segregate and divide people into groups for ease of classification and to help us make sense of the world. Or you have the others with one foot in each camp, society and genetics create gender. For me, I'm probably on the side of the latter, the fence sitters.

Whilst genetics can influence the development of certain body parts as well as the levels of certain hormones, social forces also influence our ideas about how women and men are supposed to act. For example, it is widely accepted that depression seems to have a genetic component, but that environmental factors will shape the expression of the depression. The person may have a genetic predisposition, but unless they experience a particular environmental condition, they will not develop depression. If gender was only genetic then we would have a lot less variety within each gender, and if it was only social then we would see siblings or twins of the same gender express their gender in similar ways (which does not always happen). Gender is simply too complex to favour one influencing factor and reject another.

However in general, humans do not like complexity. We like things to be simple, straightforward and easy to classify. In fact, we like things to be so simple that on first meeting with a stranger our brain instantly recognises the sex and race of the person we're meeting. From there, we make our own judgements as to what this means, based on our prejudices (or lack thereof). We're looking for meaning, for clues on how we should interact with this person, whether we should be friendly, or on guard. Most of these judgements occur subconsciously or unconsciously, without us even realising.

Yet based on what we've just learnt about the complexity of gender, these superficial judgements may be incorrect. How many times have you met someone, or even passed them on the street, and wondered, "Was that a man or a woman"? How did you feel? Were you perplexed? Curious? Uncomfortable? If so, you're probably not alone. Most of us get uneasy if we can't understand something, or if it doesn't fit into our perception of the world around us. In the case of an androgynous stranger, they don't easily fit into the social classification of what a woman or a man is supposed to look like. They float somewhere in between. Therefore your brain doesn't know how to handle it.

Most people view gender as consisting of two options, woman or man. Both are mutually exclusive and different to one another. Whole industries have been developed which address gender in this way. Books have been written, seminars delivered, consulting services provided, all around the concept that men are men, and women are women. One lives on Mars and the other lives on Venus. There is no overlap.

However, I need to clarify (even if you've probably figured it out already) that I'm not one of those people. I think this is an extremely simplistic view and one which is, well, offensive to everyone.

For me, gender does not only have two options. Instead, my concept of gender exists along a spectrum. This spectrum has hyper-masculine characteristics at one end, and hyper-feminine characteristics at the other. Both versions are the exaggerated and emphasised ideals of what it means to be masculine or feminine.

Hyper-Masculine   Hyper-Feminine

In the most common way of looking at gender, we would replace hyper-masculine with "male" and substitute hyper-feminine with "female". There would not be a line joining the two, they would exist as separate points. This view of gender just does not sit well with me. I simply have to look at how my partner and I display gender in our own ways to realise that within our society some boys display "female traits" (like expressing emotion comfortably) and some girls display "male traits" (such as being competitive and direct).

The spectrum perspective of gender accounts for this by enabling individuals to be placed at various points along the continuum. Some would be closer to the masculine end of the spectrum, whilst still showing feminine traits. Whilst others would be closer to the feminine end yet still display masculine qualities. There would also be people who sit smack bang in the middle of the spectrum with a balance of both, as well as others at the polar positions, with only feminine or masculine traits in their character.

Unfortunately, the gender spectrum is not as popular as the two-separate-genders approach and this has led to strong stereotypes around what it means to fit into the box marked "woman" or the box marked "man". How often have we heard a little girl described as "bossy", only to see her withdraw and become less forthright? Or a boy acting up and getting into a fight because he was called a "sissy". Or a man hiding his emotions because "real men don't cry". Or a woman being told she is too aggressive and not nurturing enough in the workplace.

These stereotypes of what it means to belong in a box might make it easier for our brains to understand the world around us, but they can also be incredibly damaging. We've all heard the insults "he's playing like a girl" or "stop being such a girl" when describing someone who isn't performing at the expected masculine level. This type of insult is meant to offend the person it's directed to because being a girl is seen as something less, something undervalued. A video campaign went viral in 2014 after it highlighted the power of those words; "Like A Girl". In this video, a group of people (who appear to be aged from early teens to early 20s) were asked to perform activities such as running, fighting or throwing a ball like a girl, the outcome was sobering. These people started to run daintily, flinging their limbs around, sashaying their hips, swishing their hair, flapping their hands and generally depicting a feeble effort. The video asks the viewer "when did doing something "like a girl" become an insult?", challenging us to change the stereotypes society holds around what girls can and cannot do. This video was so well received that it was even shown at the American Super Bowl. Check out the hashtag #LikeAGirl to see the amazing response this video had on social media.

Whilst you're on YouTube checking out the Like A Girl video, I encourage you to watch the videos created by The Representation Project. These wonderful videos highlight the need for better representation of both genders beyond the stereotypes depicted and reinforced by the media. Whilst some areas of the media are improving (the Like A Girl video playing at the Super Bowl is one example), there are still plenty of people who say media doesn't influence real life. Instead, they propose that it's actually real life that influences the media. They believe that media simply reports on innate human behaviour, rather than the media influencing the behaviour of the genders through the messages it sends out. Once again, we are back at the genetics vs society debate.

Throughout this book, I will be presenting research on the behaviours depicted by men and women as identified through scientific investigation. I will also be discussing characteristics and traits which I have witnessed and experienced when working with women and men in the masculine industries. However, I want to be very clear that just because the research obtains a certain finding, or just because I have observed a pattern of behaviour, it does not mean it is true across all people who identify with that gender. Remember the gender spectrum concept. Remember the scientists and I have been influenced by our own social environments. Remember we all hold our concepts, prejudices and biases about what it means to be woman or man. And especially remember the results and observations only give us an indication of what exists at a certain moment in time, with a certain sample of people. The research outcomes do not mean the findings have always been true, nor do they necessarily dictate what will be true in the future.

So now you might be thinking why did I even write this book if everything about gender is so uncertain?

Because during times of uncertainty we need to take stock of all the information available to us. We can use this uncertainty to redefine who we want to be. When we believe things are true and certain, there is nothing to challenge and hence, nothing to change. By not having clear answers we are in exciting times where we can influence the future development towards answers and understanding.

Throughout the coming chapters I will present you information about the uncertainties, showcase current research and explore the gender cultures as they currently exist within the masculine industries. I want you to gain a deeper understanding of why the masculine industries are the way they are. To understand the motivations which drive people to behave in a certain way and to gain awareness about your own behaviours. Irrespective of who you work with, male or female, if you can understand the motives behind their behaviour, and understand a little about what they are thinking, you can influence them. That influence can then be used to build a relationship or get an outcome that you need. Simultaneously, being aware of your own thoughts, feelings and behaviours will enable you to have better self-control over how you respond to different situations. It is this type of social and self-awareness that will help you achieve success in your professional and personal worlds.

If we remain unaware of the motivations and thoughts other people hold we run the risk of getting frustrated, annoyed and even angry when they act in a way which we don't like. Then, if we are also unaware of our own thoughts, emotions and behaviours we are more likely to react in a way which will get the other person angry too. It is a vicious cycle. That person may even continue to do the things that annoy you because they are getting a reaction from you. In other words, if you're not in control of your own emotions or behaviour, then someone else will be. This person, who creates an emotional reaction in you, is essentially controlling you without you being aware.

So I ask you - are you aware of your behaviour? Of your thoughts? Of your preferences?

Or do you just exist?

Do you just go through life, participating but not critically engaging? Do you not reflect, not question your own motives, or the motives of others, not observing your behaviour like an outsider or challenging yourself why you think a certain thought or perceive the world in a certain way?

Because if you just exist, you are likely operating in a way that you are not conscious of. Your thoughts and beliefs may be 'gendered' without you even realising it, and you may hold biases about yourself and other people which you could be completely unaware of.

Yet imagine if you realised why you were doing what you were doing? What if you realised that maybe your own thoughts weren't actually your own, they were the product of a social expectation, an experience you once had, a comment from another person or maybe even your genetics? What if your own biases or prejudices suddenly became conscious and you were aware of what was driving your behaviour? Would it change your thoughts? Would you decide to act differently?

As you progress through this book please keep this concept in mind. It is about presenting the reality for many people along with research findings to help us become aware of what we are all doing to contribute to the culture of the masculine industries. Also, please keep in mind that gender is not as simple as being born with a penis or a vagina. Nor does one or the other dictate your behaviours or preferences indefinitely. Remember that society and environment can influence the expression of gender and that there are certain expectations we all hold about what it is to be a "female" or a "male". This book will help you to begin exploring why we do what we do, so you can continue your own journey to greater awareness and success.

Getting Personal with Gender Diversity

"After living with their dysfunctional behaviour for so many years (a sunk cost if ever there was one), people become invested in defending their dysfunctions rather than changing them." — Marshall Goldsmith

Diversity, particularly gender diversity, is a very personal issue for everyone. No one is excluded from this debate. Therefore, the conversation can be an uncomfortable one for many people. It challenges the existing social structures and often challenges a person's perception of their self and how this self fits into the world around them. In the world of psychology, we refer to someone's understanding of their "self" and how they fit into the world as a schema. A schema can be described as a cognitive network which helps organise and interpret information from the world around us. Schemas bias us towards information which confirm and reinforce the information and perceptions already contained in our mental images and avoids the information which challenges these schemas. It's like our little brains have selective hearing and selective attention. The reason this occurs is that the world is a confusing place filled with lots of information entering our brains at any one moment in time. Schemas are the brain's way of handling this heavy data load whilst trying to make sense of it all.

I like to think of this process as a filing system, with an overworked administrator who receives a never-ending stream of data files each day in their in-tray. The flow of data files is constant, and the poor administrator only has time to scan the title of each file and direct it to a filing cabinet which they think is relevant. This filing cabinet represents a mental schema. Unfortunately though, titles can be misleading, and because there is no time for the administrator to read the contents of the file, some files get placed in incorrect cabinets. Over time the filing cabinets of certain topics (i.e. certain schemas) begin to fill up and get bigger, and each time a similar topic arrives on the desk the administrator immediately thinks of the biggest filing cabinet (because it's so prominent) and directs the file in that direction. This causes a bias towards this particular filing cabinet, which gets bigger and bigger over time. Unfortunately, in this office size matters and the larger the filing cabinet the more correct and valid we think the content within it is.

Sounding a little abstract? Well, let me give you a real-life example. Consider if you will an older male manager, let's call him John, who grew up in a world where men go to work and women stay home to tend family and household chores. John has a schema (with a filing administrator) around the gendered roles of men and women. As he grew, John received messages from external influences (i.e. data files), such as media, family, friends, that reinforced this schema (i.e. that filled the filing cabinets of "Men's Roles" and "Women's Roles"). He married a woman, who adopted the household chores and child-rearing as her duty, which were the same gender roles to which he had been exposed to as a child. Again, this information is directed to the filing cabinet marked "Gender Roles", which is now bursting at the seams and requires more drawers. John works in an industry that is filled with men whose wives also stay at home to mind children and tend to household duties. The filing cabinet keeps expanding as the schema becomes more established. It is important to note that John does not consciously realise he has any gender schemas. All of this filling is happening at an unconscious level in his mind.

One day, the company where John works appoints a female executive, who is unmarried and does not have children. This piece of information enters John's brain, but the brain's administrator cannot figure out which filing cabinet to put this information in because it has never before received a file titled "Female Executive". It's had files titled "Female Mother", "Female Household Chores" and "Female Assistant" and its seen files titled "Male Executive" and "Male Breadwinner", but certainly not a file that combines these two ideas. The unconscious administrator does not know where to put this file as it doesn't fit with the way John normally perceives the world.

This ill-fitting file causes anguish and discomfort for his brain (we call this cognitive dissonance) on an unconscious level. John does not know that this is what's happening in his brain, but he does realise that he's unhappy with a female executive joining his company.

John is unaware that his displeasure is coming from the cognitive dissonance caused by the fact that his mental schemas around gender roles are creating an unconscious bias towards this woman executive. All John knows is that it's not "right" to have a female executive, she won't be as competent as a male executive and that he is displeased to work with her.

Therefore, these unconscious feelings (i.e. unconscious biases) subtly influence John's behaviour towards the female executive. Without realising it, he may speak over her in meetings, forget to include her in group emails about important information, and score her more harshly when her 360 feedback review questionnaire lands in his inbox. Without realising all of this, John's brain and its unconscious biases are trying to ignore or remove the confusing information that is a "Female Executive".

At the very root of it, I believe it is these gender schemas, cognitive dissonance and unconscious bias which I believe is the cause of the slow advancement of women in masculine industries. The diversity, equality and inclusion conversation challenges many people's schemas of what it means to be a man and a woman and the roles we're meant to play in society. However, if we are ever going to improve gender equality we need to admit we all hold these biases and schemas and get comfortable with feeling uncomfortable when these are challenged.

To achieve this we need to stop being so politically correct. Too often we are worried about saying or doing the wrong thing that we keep our mouths shut. Political correctness has given us a code of conduct for what is "right or wrong" but has prevented us from sharing with the world how we really feel. I think this is risky. Whilst we must always treat others with respect and acceptance, we must be cautious about not sharing the things that make us uncomfortable. We must find a way to communicate our discomfort with things that challenge our schemas without being bigoted, racist, sexist or judgemental of any other differences we see. We must do this because learning to keep our mouths shut has only achieved small steps into removing prejudices against others, but it has not eliminated them entirely. Rather, the thoughts people have which lead to discrimination have been forced below the surface of behaviour and translated into covert discrimination and unconscious bias. Political correctness, legislation and laws have gotten us a little way along the journey, but they can't continue as the only method for improving equality and inclusion. We need to be brave enough, accepting enough and open enough (all scary things) to be honest about our true thoughts, become aware of any biases we hold and learn how to communicate in a way which is kind and compassionate to the people we hold these biases against. We must be truthful of the fears we have, the confusion we hold and the discomfort we experience when presented with people we are biased towards. On the flip side, the people who biases are held against or those trying to eliminate biases will need to find a way to listen to these open conversations in a way that does not blame and is not angry at the biased individual. It will be just as hard for people on all sides of the equation to become comfortable with this sort of a conversation.

Yet it's important we must find a way. Particularly in the masculine industries who, as of recently have been setting strategies to try and entice more women into their organisations. Because whilst a strategy might exist at the top level of an organisation, the reality of how it plays out in the field and the lower levels or an organisation are very different. Numerous times I've had male leaders secretly confess they hate the idea of gender quotas. When I ask whether they've voiced this opinion to others in the business they look aghast and say "no way, I could never do that". For them, the idea of telling the truth is too politically incorrect and would cast them as a pariah in an organisation that is trying to achieve greater gender diversity. However, because their thoughts are never voiced, their internal ideas are never challenged and they are never educated on a different point of view. Their schemas remain the same, their unconscious bias remains unchecked and their behaviours are displayed in ways they may not even be aware of.

Because of all of this, I am a fan of having the hard conversation. I love it when a manager tells me they don't like quotas, or when a supervisor admits to not liking women in their crew. I like it, not because I agree with them, but because they told the truth. It is the truth I can work with, lies and mistruths I cannot. When someone tells the truth it means one of two things, they either trust you, or they're testing you. You can usually tell which one they are, based on your prior relationship or with a few follow up questions like "can you tell me more about why you feel that way". If they're testing you their response will be full of arrogance and road blocks. If they trust you they will explain why. It is with this person that the conversation is easier and enlightening for both parties. With the other person (who is testing you) you can still engage in the conversation, but you should enter with a questioning mind, not a judgemental approach. Just because they said they don't believe in quotas, or that they don't like women in the crew, doesn't mean they're an awful person, they just have a different perspective. I've tried this approach previously with many people and have wound up having great conversations which have enlightened us both. In some cases, I have provided them with information they'd never previously considered and which has led them to view the world differently from that day forward. I have also received great insight into the roadblocks of gender equality which has assisted me in shaping my approach. Difference does not have to be a source of conflict; it can be the wellspring of growth and change.

Gender Diversity in Australia

"Diversity in the world is a basic characteristic of human society, and also the key condition for a lively and dynamic world as we see today." – Jintao Hu

Country Culture

The culture of a country influences the way in which people experience their day-to-day life. It influences politics, workplaces, institutions and to a certain degree, individuals. Geert Hofstede has spent many years identifying and distinguishing culture of over 70 countries. Hofstede compares cultures between countries across six dimensions: Power Distance, Individualism versus Collectivism, Masculinity versus Femininity, Uncertainty Avoidance, Long-Term Orientation and Indulgence versus Restraint. His work has identified Australia as having low power distance meaning superiors are accessible, communication is informal and information is shared freely. On the Individualism versus Collectivism dimension, we have been found to be a highly individualistic country where people look after themselves and their direct family only. We are regarded as having a masculine culture with a competitive, assertive approach that uses material rewards for success and endorses the "winner takes all" approach. Australians have an intermediate approach to Uncertainty Avoidance and are regarded as neither avoidant nor accepting of uncertainty and ambiguity. We score very low on Long-

Term Orientation which means we are prone to hold on to old ways and traditions, view societal change with suspicion, have a small propensity to save for the future and prefer to make short-term decisions to achieve quick results. Finally, we have been found to be quite indulgent and will satisfy our impulses and desires with the aim of having fun in life. In other words, we are a collection of selfish, masculine individuals who don't like change but want life to always be fun.

Now compare this to the cultures of the top 5 countries (i.e. the Nordic countries) that consistently perform well across gender equality statistics. In the case of the Masculine versus Feminine dimension, all the Nordic countries have very low masculine scores. This means their culture is regarded as feminine which values well-being over status, solidarity and consensus among members. Another interesting difference between Australia and the top five countries for gender equality is in their Individualism score. Australia has a very high Individualism score of 90 out of a 100, whereas the top five have a combined average of 61.4 out of 100. This means that whilst they are still mildly individualistic they display more collectivist tendencies compared to Australian culture.

It is these two differences in culture that make me question the success of quotas in Australia. If the Nordic countries have a culture which supports egalitarianism, consensus and equality, the notion of creating a gender quota might seem sensible. It fits with the cultural notions of what is fair. Combine this with a reduced focus on individualism and I begin to wonder whether people in Nordic cultures feel less strongly about getting one's self ahead and more focused on ensuring the group is OK. In my mind, these two factors intuitively make sense for the support and success of diversity and for enforcing quotas. Their culture expects things to be fair and presumably is comfortable to introduce measures to address inequality wherever it may exist. However, I do acknowledge that my understanding of the cultures and Nordic ways of life and legislation are limited and this is simply my musings.

Nonetheless, it does make me ponder the cultural ramifications of the successful adoption of gender quotas in the Australian context. When we belong to a group, the culture of that group will have an impact on our values, beliefs and norms and influence our behaviour and thoughts, often without us even recognising it. If we exist in the Australian culture, then our unconscious thoughts and overt behaviours are likely to mirror this culture, which may I remind you, according to Hofstede's research is masculine, highly individualistic, short-term focused and resistant to change. So let's take a deeper look into how Quotas might work in the Australian context.

Quotas

Let me be honest with you. I was hesitant to include the discussion of quotas in this book, much like I didn't want to discuss the gender pay gap (don't worry, we are going to explore that below), but as I've been putting together this research I realise it is unavoidable if you're writing about gender equality. These topics are probably the most contentious when it comes to gender equality and as such, really can't be ignored.

So let me lay my cards on the table … gender quotas make me uneasy.

Whilst I am not fully opposed to quotas (I recognise that what gets measured gets managed), I do not believe quotas are the top solution for achieving gender equality. The reason behind my view ties in with the previous discussion around the psychology of people and the culture of Australia.

Forcing compulsory gender quotas, without implementing any other equality and inclusion initiatives is going to challenge the very notion of the Australian culture. We will be asking our nation, who does not really like to change, to make big changes to their identity. With quotas, we are asking them to accept and embrace femininity when historically it has been proudly masculine. We will be asking individualistic individuals to take a step back and let others (who may be judged unworthy) to take a seat at the table. And we will be planning for the long-term prosperity of our society when we would much prefer to enjoy the fruits of today.

I believe quotas cause immense cognitive dissonance for many leaders. Why? Because you're asking a leader to aim for an end goal that they may not inherently agree with, but to which you are going to reward or punish them based on their achievement of that end goal. You are asking them to strive for something which they may not actually want. They will be externally punished if they don't achieve the goal (i.e. lack of performance bonus, reduced career progression, etc.), but they will be internally punished if they do achieve the goal (i.e. through the cognitive dissonance of doing something they don't want to do). It's a conflicting situation that makes them want to run towards the objective (i.e. achieve the target) but away from the items which cause mental discomfort (i.e. increasing the percentage of women). It's no wonder people are uncomfortable about quotas and unsurprising gender equality is making very slow progress in Australia.

As discussed the Nordic countries of the European Union are top performers when it comes to gender statistics, particularly in the World Economic Forum Global Gender Gap Report. Iceland, Finland, Norway, Sweden and Denmark occupy the top five positions of gender equality against the Global Gender Gap Report metrics. These same countries also have the highest percentage of women representatives in national parliaments within the European Union as outlined by the report provided by the European Union Directorate General for Internal Policies. Yet, it may come as a surprise that only three of the five countries have gender quotas. Finland and Denmark do not have quotas but still manage to have 42.5% and 39.1% women respectively in their national parliaments (as reported in 2011). This same report concludes that quotas are not a necessary or sufficient condition for a high level of female representation.

This has been my suspicion for a number of years, that quotas will not be the solution to our gender equality problem. My belief is that a country's culture plays a larger part in gender equality than quotas do. And this is where attention, resources and time should be placed if we want to improve gender equality in Australia.

Therefore, if governments, institutions and even companies decide to bring in quotas they should only do so with strong consideration of the cultural context. It will be important to use a multi-faceted approach that addresses individual psychological and social-cultural considerations, along with the introduction of quotas. Without this holistic approach, I believe the success of quotas will be limited in

Australia and we will not make fast gains towards achieving equality.

Gender Wage Gap

Writing about the statistics of equality, diversity, women in non-traditional industries and the gender wage gap always makes me a mixture of angry and depressed. Angry because I can't believe its 2016 and we're still dealing with this crap, and depressed because the pace of change is slow, non-existent or in some cases, regressing.

The gender wage gap is one of those topics that really pisses me off. I mean, how on earth does this still exist? It's nonsensical. Equal pay for equal work. It's really not a difficult concept to grasp.

Yet, it appears that for some reason or another, we just haven't got there yet.

When talking about gender statistics and wage gaps it's important to recognise the history of where we have come from. At the beginning of this century, women were paid one half or two-thirds of a male's salary. It was commonplace and widely accepted that women were worth less, even if they were performing the same job as a man. Unfortunately even after the Australian Conciliation and Arbitration Commission granted "equal pay for equal work" in 1969 we know that the reality of this ruling has never come to fruition. Therefore, whilst the conversation around the gender wage gap is old news, it does not mean its importance has eroded over the years. We need to continue questioning and challenging the assumptions which are causing the gender wage gap and not rest until true wage equality is achieved for everyone.

For the past 20 years, the wage gap in Australia has remained fairly stable, fluctuating between a low of 14.9% in 2004, up to a new record high of 18.8% in November 2014. Even with the recent renewed focus on gender equality in our media, institutions and organisations, we haven't made a big shift in reducing it. In fact, in 2014 we recorded our highest pay gap ever and have only just shown a slight dip the following year. I'm happy about the statistic tracking downwards but I'm not going to get too excited as we have seen this fluctuation for decades.

The Workplace Gender Equality Agency explains that the wage gap is calculated from full-time weekly earnings before tax and with the exclusion of overtime, bonus payments, discretionary pay, superannuation, other allowances and share allowances. However, the ABS warns their wage gap data does not "take into account a range of compositional differences, for example, differences in occupation or hours worked" (ABS, 2015). It is this point that causes many people to doubt the validity of the gender wage gap. When trawling through the various comments on the internet regarding the gender wage gap it is common to see comments denouncing its existence:

"Are we saying that a childcare worker or a retail employee should be paid the same as a teacher or police officer? Men do all of the dirty, dusty, hazardous and physical jobs. This is why there is a pay gap." – Pedro2000

"In fact men are still doing the same dangerous, dirty, risky jobs they have always done. They continue to produce and manage our power, water, sewerage, buildings, fuel, food, transport and much more. If women want to do the same jobs for the same money, they can." – Snufkin

"Statistics are a wonderful thing. The case presented does not agree with my reality. Jobs pay what jobs pay. The statistics are more a reflection on the choices people make than anything else." – Sue D

"People do go to great lengths to externalise their failures and underachievement, don't they." – Mike J

"Theoretical nonsense. Again, I have experience in this area and I can honestly tell you that any suggestion of some great conspiracy against women in terms of pay rates is, in my experience, void of any merit whatsoever. Failing evidence of that, you (and many feminists) suggest that it must be "socialisation". I.e. that women have no choice and society is forcing them to take less pay." - Derby

Whilst on the face of it, some of these comments are true: Men are the ones who currently occupy the majority of jobs in power, water, buildings, transport and it is true that "jobs pay what jobs pay" (so insightful!). But what these people fail to see is the deeper reasoning behind why this is the case.

For example, I have worked many years in mining and construction and have seen a wide range of jobs being conducted in both industries. They can be physically demanding and risky; there is absolutely no doubt about that. Fortunately all organisations worth their salt have implemented processes to manage and where possible eliminate the risks. Whilst it pains me to say there are undoubtedly organisations which still permit (i.e. turn a blind eye to) risky behaviours in the pursuit of profits, there are other ways to navigate such dangers. Methods for 'engineering out' risk, eliminating it all together or putting controls in place are all common practices for mining and construction organisations. Therefore, I do not buy the argument that all jobs in mining and construction should be paid more than other jobs because of the risk involved.

Here is my reason: I grew up with a mother who worked in a nursing home, I now have a sister-in-law who also does this job and I have cousins who are nurses in Emergency Response clinics in some of the rougher regions of Australia. Each of these women are placed in a risky environment every time they go to work. My mother would come home with dark bruises and scratches from the residents with dementia; she would be spat on, verbally abused and struck. She experienced shoulder injuries from manually handling the heavy lifting equipment, and moving the overweight patients. She also had a colleague thrown across a room by a resident causing such extensive injuries she was unable to nurse again. My cousin the ER nurse is regularly threatened, struck and abused by alcohol and/or drug-fuelled patients admitted to the clinic and has had her life threatened on more than one occasion. Another reports punches being thrown at nurses and withdrawing alcoholics trying to strangle staff. Being a nurse is not a nice, safe, fluffy job. It is physically demanding (you're on your feet all day), its dirty (you're dealing with people's faeces, vomit, blood, saliva and pus) and it can be downright dangerous. So dangerous in fact, that research conducted by The University of Melbourne found that mental health care nurses were more likely to be assaulted than police. You can't tell me that mining and construction are inherently riskier and hence workers in these industries deserve to be paid more.

Now someone who would like to refute my argument might point to the statistics of workplace fatalities. This is a fair point. The male-dominated industries (transport, postal & warehousing, agriculture, forestry & fishing, construction and mining) are ranked highest when it comes to workplace fatalities. However, I cannot accept that all of these deaths occurred due to the inherently risky nature of the job. Most of these industries are governed by strict health and safety laws and standards. However, in 2014 these industries had a combined total of 138 workplace fatalities. Whereas the feminine industries (healthcare & social assistance, education & training, administrative & support services) had a combined number of 6 workplace fatalities in 2014. So while it is obvious that masculine industries report more deaths in their workplaces, I am not convinced it is due to the inherent risks of the job, but perhaps caused by something else. Dean Laplonge explores the concept of gender and safety in his work and touches on this in his book *So You Think You're Tough* (2014). Laplonge suggests the increased accident and fatality rate might actually be due to the masculinised culture within these workplaces that encourages risk, machoism and aggression. These characteristics can lead to a disregard for the rules, a "she'll be right mate" attitude and the acceptance of cutting corners to achieve goals. I don't know about you, but I don't think we should be rewarding this kind of attitude with an inflated salary.

There is also the argument that men work longer hours than women and hence this accounts for the gender wage gap. Now I have absolutely no issue with people getting paid more if they work more. That is just logical. However, I think accounting for the gender wage gap through overtime and longer working hours is too simplistic. Take for example graduate starting salaries. The Graduate Careers Australia's Graduate Starting Salaries data identified that of 18 fields of study completed by graduates in 2013, 14 of these had male graduates earning more than female graduates. The top industries for this disparity were architecture and building. The four industries which had female graduates earning a larger starting salary compared to their male counterparts included pharmacy, engineering, computer sciences and earth sciences (which had the largest gap). What I don't understand about this data is how can you possibly pay two graduates in the same role at a different rate? Aren't they all grads, aren't they all starting at the same level? I am also going to hedge a bet that grads work similar hours, irrespective of their gender, so how is this difference justifiable? Truly, I'm intrigued.

The American Sociological Review conducted research into the relationship between longer working hours (referred to as "overwork") on the gender wage gap (Cha & Weeden, 2014). They concluded that overwork accounted for about 10% of the gender wage gap. They clarified this claim by stating that over the period of their research focus, there was very little change between the number of men who overworked and the number of women who overworked, across time. What had seemed to have changed is the way this overwork was remunerated and rewarded. They also suggest that the ability to overwork is only made possible by "the support of other household members, usually women". Whilst they found evidence to suggest that men working longer hours contributes to the gender wage gap, they only recognise this as a symptom, not a cause of the inequality problems. In their concluding remarks, they refer to the organisational expectation of working long hours as another way which "builds on and perpetuates old forms of gender inequality". In other words, society (and the organisations within it) is guilty of creating structures, cultures and remuneration benefits which can only be accessed by men.

Therefore, the two arguments which are commonly used to discredit the gender wage gap are in essence superfluous to the entire discussion. Yes, the types of roles which people undertake along with the number of hours they work will have an impact on someone's remuneration. There is no denying it, but that is not what the gender gap is demonstrating. It is highlighting the inequality which still exists within our society. Certain skills are regarded more highly than others. Moving dirt and building things is seen as more valuable than influencing the development of the next generation or tending to a critically ill person. The former get paid extraordinarily well, whilst the others get paid a pittance in comparison.

The gender wage gap also makes us question why women aren't drawn to these higher paying jobs and industries. We should use the statistic as a clue, a hint towards finding out what is really going on. When we start to look closer we begin to notice that in the professions of engineering, women might start out getting paid more than men, but over time they are the ones who end up leaving the profession in the greater percentage. We also notice that the higher up we go in an organisation, the bigger the wage gap is likely to be between the women (if there's any up there at all) and the men. The men end up getting paid more. So the next time someone wants to discredit the gender wage gap, tell them they are totally missing the point. The gender wage gap represents far more than the amount on someone's pay cheque. It is highlighting a deeper level of inequality in our society.

PART 2

Women's Business

"I write for those women who do not speak, for those who do not have a voice because they were so terrified, because we are taught to respect fear more than ourselves. We've been taught that silence would save us, but it won't."

Audre Lorde

"You work where?"

It's a common response when you tell people you work in mining /construction/engineering/oil and gas (or any other traditionally masculine industry for that matter). Unfortunately, it still seems to surprise people when I tell them I work in the mines, or in construction. People are shocked when they hear that a woman is doing a man's job, or even working in a man's industry. The shock is compounded when the female in question doesn't fit the stereotype of what the person thought women in these industries would look like. Apparently, it's strange that a girl who likes nail art also enjoys getting grubby when at work.

The second question that seems to follow is "what's it like?" People are curious to know what it's like to be a woman working with mainly men. They wonder about the culture of the workplace and how I would fit in. I tell them it's usually a very masculine place to work, but that different industries (for example underground coal mining versus open cut iron ore mining) are different in their expression of this masculinity. I explain how much I love working with blokes, most of them are fun, respectful and kind, others will challenge you (which can also be quite fun) and then there is the remaining few who will be condescending narcissistic assholes. I explain that some sites have a terrible culture when it comes to women but there are others where being a woman doesn't make a difference. I tell them in the places I've worked humour is king, being direct and straightforward is valued and demonstrating confidence (even if you don't feel it) is a must.

In a survey conducted by *The Blue Collared Woman* (The BCW) the following comments were used by other women to describe the different masculine industries they worked in, including mining, construction, oil and gas, rail, engineering and agriculture. They described the culture of their own industry as:

- Productive, solutions focused, sometimes aggressive;
- Alpha male;
- Busy, evolving, challenging;
- Dynamic, tough and fast paced;
- Hard working, fast moving, but also still an element of tradition;
- Rugged, hyper-masculine, mostly laid back, pretty exciting;
- Male dominated, stressful, tiring, intense;
- Hectic;
- Geeky, innovative;
- A challenge, but fabulously rewarding;
- Competitive, commercial, high pressure;
- Male dominated and tough;
- Down to earth, high pressure, male dominated;
- Light-hearted;
- Informal;
- Macho. Poor communication;
- Hard, complicated, frustrating and well paid;
- Relatively inclusive if you work hard;
- A lot less scary than what you think.

What I love most about these comments is the similarity between experiences. These responses were collected anonymously via a call out on social media. It is likely that the women who answered did so of their own accord and the majority may not have known one another. The largest portion of women who responded worked out in the field (52.17%), with the remaining working in corporate offices (39.13%) or site-based office roles (30.43%). The roles undertaken by these women were diverse and included trades, engineering, geology, environment, administration, project management, human resources, operations, supervisory, community and marketing. So even at different levels of the organisation and in different professions, the experiences of women in masculine workplaces seemed to share a commonality. As mentioned, it is this commonality in experiences that spurred me to write this book.

When reviewing these cultural descriptions at a macro level you get the impression the masculine industries are downright difficult. It looks to be a lot of hard work with very little fun. So why do women want to work in a place like this? Well it all comes down to four main themes: (1) the types of projects you get to work on and the tangible outcomes these lead to, (2) the challenges and experiences you encounter which help you grow as a person, (3) the people you get to work with and the impact you can have personally, and finally (4) the remuneration benefits of a high salary.

There is no doubt many of the masculine industries have long-lasting impacts on society. They construct the roads and buildings which are around for generations, they provide the resources to grow economies and increase productivity and they produce the items which modern society has come to rely on. As one Engineer put it "I work on end products that improve people's lives. Engineering can be exciting when problem-solving and thinking about new products for the market." These industries are often project-based, situated in interesting locations and require energy to keep up with deadlines. A

Human Resource professional in the construction industry loves this side of her job, "I enjoy the fast pace of projects, and being a part of contributing to society through the type of work we do – e.g. social infrastructure".

They also present you with many exciting experiences, some of which are completely inaccessible to the majority of the population. "It's different" states a woman who has worked in mining, manufacturing, construction and energy. "You get exposure to so many interesting things normally reserved only for the guys". "I do things with my hands and brain that a lot can't!!! It's an art!!!" says another woman employed as a Journeyman Steamfitter. In my own roles, I've had some wonderful experiences, seen some amazing locations, and learned some valuable lessons about myself professionally and personally. None of which would have been possible if I hadn't been working in a masculine industry. As one solar electrical tradeswoman put it, "it's the vastness of opportunities across the industry" that keeps us passionate about the industries we work in.

However, it's not just about the jobs and the experiences that keep us interested. A big part of the drawcard is the people we get to work with. Many women report having a preference for working with men or having grown up surrounded by men. Many of the female respondents said they found men to be "generally more honest and easy to work with", "a lot of fun", "down to earth", "say what they feel and the clarity is very helpful" and that there tends to be more "comradery between teams" and "rarely any bitchiness". One engineer even made a quip that there's "(n)ot much talk of hair or fashion or babies, talking crap is encouraged, so is general idiocy and horseplay, which I like". Personally, I can relate to all of these comments. I have always enjoyed working with men which I suppose may have developed due to a childhood surrounded by boys. Whilst I didn't have any siblings most of my neighbours were boys, my closest cousins were boys and I always wished I'd had an older brother rather than being an only child. I loved that when we were together we were loud and rowdy, grubby from building cubbies in the bush, running around being active and were always pitting ourselves against one another physically. I also remember that laughter and jokes played a huge part in how we engaged with one another.

This theme of humour and fun also came across in the responses other women provided about working with men. There is something very enjoyable and unifying about the good-hearted jokes and the jocularity that comes when people are comfortable with one another. Whenever I start work on a new site, or in a new team, I always know that I've been accepted when the guys start making jokes in my presence. It becomes even more obvious that I've been accepted as one-of-the-crew when I'm on the receiving end of their jokes!

The final theme which appeared in the women's responses was the financial and lifestyle benefits that can be found in the industry. For those who enjoy working on a Fly-In Fly-Out (FIFO) roster the balance between work and social life can be achieved. Various rosters exist in the industry, from working 8 days on to having 6 off, or even time rosters of 2 weeks on 2 weeks off, to the more traditional rosters of 4 weeks on and 1 off. The tricky thing with these rosters is that not a single one of them will suit everyone and all of them will suit someone. The success of FIFO rosters, and reaping their benefits, comes down to finding one that suits your particular circumstances. Each of them will bring their own challenges and financial rewards. Nonetheless, many of the roles in masculine industries are very well paid compared to other industries (as discussed in the chapter on the gender wage gap) and this was reported as a big incentive for many women.

It's not all fun

Whilst there are lots of reasons to enjoy working in the masculine industries, the reality is not all tea and biscuits. Sometimes there are unique challenges we women encounter that the majority of blokes don't have to endure. These challenges certainly don't mean we hate our jobs or the people we work with, but they do require special consideration and navigation to ensure they don't become our undoing.

These challenges can include being stereotyped because of your gender, being the subject of degrading comments/rumours, being talked over in meetings, fighting hard to be accepted as a valued team member by male colleagues, the stress of monitoring your behaviour 24/7 for fear of judgement, having your ideas ignored only to be repeated by someone else later on, the absence of suitable role models you can relate to, encountering sexual advances/harassment at work, dealing with amenities unsuitable for women (or complete lack of), finding uniforms that fit correctly, receiving condescending comments like "good girl", "love", etc., being questioned about childcare or your intention to have kids, having your appearance scrutinised and commented on, having your abilities doubted because you're a female and dealing with an environment/individuals with heightened levels of aggression. Phew, it's a mouthful! Yet this list is a compilation of the challenges experienced by many women across a range of industries but is in no way completely representative of the experiences of all women. There will, of course, be women who haven't experienced any of these challenges, some who have encountered a couple, and there will be those who have dealt with the lot and more!

I often find that when I speak about these challenges some women will debate the existence of such things. They will challenge the concept of women needing "special treatment" or "women's only" workshops and events. There is a belief that since it is not happening to them, then it doesn't exist and we're all making a big fuss over nothing. However, I do not need to experience something to know it exists. I have never been subjected to racial bias because I was born with white skin, but I know it exists for people who have brown skin. The concept is exactly the same.

It is important to recognise these challenges do exist so that we become increasingly aware of the environments we operate in. So although we should not be discouraged or fearful, I do not believe we should stick our heads in the sand, put our fingers in our ears and block out reality. I fear we have been doing this too much already by trying to fit in with the prevailing culture rather than questioning or scrutinising it.

So let's explore these challenges for women in the masculine industries to paint a realistic picture of what it's like for many women who work in them today.

Gender Stereotypes

"Are you here to take the notes love?" was the question asked of me by a middle-aged mining Superintendent. I had entered the meeting room with six big burly Mining Supervisors and Superintendents. I say "big" and "burly" because although most of the men were my height, they all seemed to take up at least twice the space I would. I knew most of the blokes in the meeting room, but unfortunately for the fella who asked the seemingly innocent question, we hadn't met yet. Little did he know I was there as a leadership consultant, who had been asked to sit in on the meeting to observe and provide feedback on the business's leaders. This little story perfectly highlights the assumptions that exist about women's roles on site. For many years the only role suitable for women to occupy in a male-dominated industry was the role of administrator or secretary. These roles, let's call them "helper" roles, were congruent with the social norms that women held only caring, supporting, second fiddle roles. Certainly, they did not hold positions which were autonomous, powerful or influential. Even today it is not uncommon to walk into the office of a mining company or construction office to be greeted by a female face on the front desk, but see no others once you step past the front partition into the back offices. As one woman in the construction industry put it "Generally I think men expect women to tend to the hygiene factors at work – e.g. making sure kitchens are clean, and events are catered, and meeting rooms are tidied up". In other words, the stereotype of woman as social giver and carer remains strong, even in a professional setting.

Whilst most organisations, particularly the larger ones, have tried to diminish this stereotype of a woman's role, gender inequality does remain in some sectors. Typically you find women clustered into the following roles in masculine industries; administration, human resources, community/marketing, and to some extent, finance and commercial. The roles of administration and human resources are populated so extensively by females that they have been referred to as "pink ghettos". The areas of engineering, project management, supervision, technical, trade, labourer, operator, manager still tend to be occupied by a male majority. Another interesting observation is that although the pink ghettos are populated by women, the leaders and managers of these departments are likely to be male. Talk about a glass ceiling on a room filled with pink decor.

The stereotype that women can't do a man's job still prevails in many sectors. Comments from women working in mining report that men "judge them (women) a lot more harsh. Women have a lot more to prove to men in the workplace especially in leadership roles. It takes ages to build credibility and not long for it to be destroyed". Another stated that "generally the more traditional roles of operating machinery and maintenance areas are still quite sexist. Geology has a more equal representation of women". There was also a theme of being patronised in their roles "older men treat us like pets, I find baby boomers threatened, some young guys are OK but some grads are total jerks", said a mining electrical engineer. Whereas a woman in construction felt "some treat you the same as the men, some treat you like their daughter or granddaughter and struggle to accept your opinion, but most of the time they are pretty good."

It is undeniable these stereotypes still exist in the workplace but I believe things are changing. Slowly. Other women are also reporting a greater acceptance of women in masculine industries. An engineer for the oil and gas industry believes this acceptance "depends largely on the personality and background of the guys as well as their exposure to women in the workplace in addition to the attitude and aptitude of the woman in question". As one woman commented about being accepted by men, "the majority is positive, usually takes them a few days to warm up to the idea once they realise she's good at her job and knows what's going on. I thought sometimes they judge women too harshly but then I realised they rip on the guys all the time too". When a carpenter was asked how she felt men responded to women at work she replied "in theory, well. In practice, sometimes less so. It isn't really acceptable these days to blatantly say that you don't support gender equality, so most men will say that it's great that women are starting out in trades. The awareness of what it actually means to be equal is still forming though. That said, some men are great at treating me as well as anyone else". It is this comment which gets to the crux of what is happening to diversity in our masculine industries. We are at the stage now where we know what is right and what is wrong, what we can say, and what we can't. But that doesn't mean the thoughts inside our heads have changed. This is the perfect example of the unconscious biases and mental schemas discussed in the earlier chapter of Getting Personal with Gender Diversity. Some people in our industries will have stereotypes and biases against women in non-traditional roles. Therefore, as women we must be aware of this and decide how we're going to handle it.

When it comes to navigating stereotypes it's important to be aware of how we are acting. We must become conscious of our behaviour and the way it is being perceived by other people, how it is affecting our relationships with others and the entire impression of women in masculine industries. It is not about changing who we are, but simply being self-aware and choosing the most suitable behaviour for each scenario with the aim of getting the best outcome. We need to be conscious of whether we are going to live up to a stereotype (of being caring, supportive, egalitarian), or whether we are going to challenge it (being direct, assertive, and (shock horror) bossy). In my opinion, there is a time and a place for them all. In some scenarios, it will suit you very well to use feminine qualities (for example if a colleague receives tragic news of a family member and is seeking comfort), whereas other times you may need to turn on the masculine qualities (such as negotiating a final price with a pushy contractor). However, it's a fine line we walk as women because we know that if we are perceived as exhibiting too many masculine behaviours, we can be penalised (in performance reviews, peer evaluations, etc.). Therefore, self-awareness is king. Know what you're doing and understand the outcome.

Being the subject of degrading comments/rumours

In most social situations, the odd one out tends to bear the most scrutiny. It could be the kid in class who gets bullied for wearing gumboots to sports class because his family doesn't have enough money for sneakers. Or the Middle Eastern guy who cops all the bomb-making, terrorist jokes at the pub. Or the girl from site who is the subject of rumours and gossip because she got drunk at the Christmas party and was seen leaving the venue with her manager. In these examples, the individuals are the minority in one way or another; socio-economic status, ethnicity, or gender.

Unfortunately, it is not uncommon for a woman to find herself the subject of on-site gossip or the recipient of degrading comments.

I once met a young female electrician who worked in an underground coal mine. As I too had done time underground I was interested in her experiences in that environment. She explained that the site she was on now was OK, but that she had only recently moved there because of a terrible experience on another site. At her previous workplace, she had struck up a flirtatious relationship with a guy on site that eventually became a sexual relationship. At the time she had felt comfortable enough with this person to take the relationship to the next level. However, after they had slept together the guy quickly changed his tune and started spreading rumours about their escapades amongst the other men at work. Sadly, this sort of information spreads like wild-fire on a site and soon this woman was being harassed by other men at work and camp soliciting her for sex. The situation became so unbearable that she quit her job and moved sites. Her parting advice to me as we went our separate ways was, "don't screw the crew".

In a similar fashion (minus the sexual rumours) another underground woman left her job for fear of reprisal from the men at work for dating one of the crew members. This woman and her partner kept their relationship secret for many, many months due to the fear of being found out and eventually left the site due to the stress it caused. This couple is now married and happily working together on another site.

Unfortunately, it's not just in the underground where this sort of conduct occurs. An Oil and Gas engineer reported she once "had one guy say some inappropriate things like joking about me showing my boobs or getting naked. I told my boss and he said he totally agreed that it wasn't cool and if it continued, we will follow up with it. Luckily it didn't." She goes on to explain how she handles the majority of degrading comments which tend to be less overt, "the usual sexist comments masked as jokes that I manage to shoot down with enough wit and brevity to make everyone else laugh and the person in question never make a stupid comment again". Another field engineer also experienced similar comments and experiences and she explains that there is "a bit of innuendo and also outright 'I'm going to watch your arse'." She goes on to explain how she handled this particular situation, "After a few days I spoke to him about it, quietly, and he was embarrassed. I left though so not sure if he changed his ways".

Harassment & Assaults

Unfortunately sometimes these off-hand degrading comments turn into more serious matters of sexual harassment. As women, we're constantly being told never to put ourselves in a position where we could be the target of an attacker. We're told not to go walking by ourselves, not to hang out with strange men, and to be careful when we engage with strangers.

But what if the very nature of our jobs requires us to do just that? What would you do, if the only way to get to the gym or the dining hall for dinner is to walk through badly lit, often secluded pathways, with groups of men hanging out in groups drinking alcohol? Or even worse, when those men yell something offensive at you, or you feel like someone is following you to your room.

I have been in exactly those situations, where everything you do is calculated and you're alert to who is around you. You choose the more brightly lit walking path, even though it's a bit longer than the dark shortcut and you adjust your gait to be more upright, broad-shouldered with fits slightly clenched to give a "don't fuck with me" impression.

Maybe I'm paranoid, or maybe I've just worked and lived in some pretty dodgy places, either way, it doesn't negate the feelings of fear I've had on occasion when working in the masculine industries.

Unfortunately, though it seems my cautiousness is not without reason. A recent report released by the National Drug Research Institute at Perth's Curtin University found that women in mining areas had a 64% increased risk of assault, a 59% increased risk of non-domestic assault and a frightening 136% increased risk of sexual assault compared to women in other areas (2015). The researchers also found that these results were not influenced by the prevalence of alcohol and therefore alcohol could not be used to explain the increase in assault risk to women in these areas. In other words, other factors (which the authors did not investigate) are responsible for the increased assaults on women in the mining industry.

Undoubtedly there would be a range of factors which contribute to the increased risk. However, I would be most interested to know how much the factors of a masculine culture, FIFO arrangements and percentage of women within the workforce would have on the statistic of assaults against women.

However, even outside of the mining industry the rate of sexual harassment is concerning. In the general population, 25% of women and 16% of men will experience sexual harassment in the workplace at some point in time (AHRC, 2012). Through interviewing for this book, I had many women recount stories of sexual harassment or even assault. Some stories I have shared with you throughout this book, whilst others I've had to leave untold due to their specific nature and the risk of exposing involved parties.

From the respondents to The BCW survey, 30% of women had reported experiencing sexual harassment. These women experienced groping, sexual requests and solicitations, sexual comments about their appearance (publically and privately), sexually explicit images, threatening and intimidating behaviour, being physically touched and even death threats.

One woman shared a particularly difficult situation where she was sexually harassed by her manager, "he asked me out every week. He told me I had to bring paperwork to his house one time when I finished a late job, he asked me to come in and see what he had to offer me. He was a different kind of creep. I've never met any man that even comes close to his scale of creepy. I never did file a harassment case against him. I was warned that my name would be blacklisted and it would be hard to find a company that would hire me".

Unfortunately, such horrifying statistics and experiences often go unreported or worse yet are not investigated by organisations when they do occur. I have been informed of cases where women have been physically and sexually threatened or assaulted whilst in the workplace, yet their employers do not take a firm stand on the matter. Rather, they have kept things hushed up and as one woman put it when discussing the cover-up of a recent sexual assault on-site "someone held the broom … another team member lifted the carpet". In other words, it was all swept under the rug.

Amenities (or complete lack of) suitable for women

When you're a second thought, don't expect things to be well planned. This is exactly the case on many mine sites that were built before any woman dared set foot within the site gates. I've worked on a site just like this where the women's toilets were a portable building placed smack bang in the middle of a quadrangle right next to the swipe in gates. Sitting on the toilet, or getting undressed to have a shower during the nights whilst you can hear the conversations of the blokes directly outside can be a little unnerving. However, I suppose the plus side of having very few women on site is that the toilet was generally empty, and you could pick any shower (out of 2) or toilet stall (out of 3) you wanted. You've got to take the small wins.

In fact, I should count myself lucky as other women have reported fighting with their Supervisor to cover up the urinals of the male-turned-female toilet block, only to have their requests rejected. The manager saw no need to have the urinal covered so dismissed the women's requests completely. Yet, these savvy women didn't take no for an answer and whilst their manager was away on leave, they enlisted a couple of the tradies on site to whip up a wooden box to fit over the urinal. These blokes didn't mind taking 10 minutes to improve the comfort and facilities for the ladies. I'm now informed this make-shift box doubles as a handy bench to lean a mirror and store hair-ties and deodorant on. The male manager who rejected the initial request remained unaware the women had improved their facilities themselves.

In this day and age, it might seem a bit ridiculous not to have female-specific amenities, but in some situations, a stinky urinal in the bathroom is the least of many women's worries. There are accounts of women having no suitable facilities in their work environment. As one electrical engineer in mining reported, they had to install a female toilet underground just for her, "at my first job working underground they made a girl's loo even though I was happy with the unisex one. This caused a lot of backlash against me, which was crap". I can imagine the backlash she received involved making her feel like she didn't belong and that she was getting special treatment for being female. Personally, my tactic for managing a lack of amenities when working underground was to only take down one airplane sized bottle of water to sip until I came back up to the surface. Fortunately, my role consisted of only going underground for approximately 4 – 6 hours at a time, but it was still a dangerous thing to do and certainly not something I endorse. It is important to take sufficient water with you underground in the event that something happens, and you are trapped down there for longer than planned. Yet even though I knew this, I was more petrified of needing to go to the toilet and having to ask the busy supervisor to get someone to drive me back to the surface so I could go tinkle. On this job I was already made to feel unwelcome and annoying and my strategy (rightly or wrongly) for coping was to place myself in a risky position in an attempt to be accepted.

Other women have reported difficulty when working on sites that don't have sanitary bins and some discussed the use of menstrual cups to enable them to work long shifts without needing to change a tampon or pad. These menstrual cups have also been a godsend for women who work in dirty jobs involving grease, dirt and other chemicals or those who have to work in remote locations. If you'd like more information on the menstrual cups, jump online to do a quick search of "Menstrual Cups Australia" in Google or visit your local chemist to see if they have some in stock.

Finding uniforms that fit correctly

This has been a tricky issue for many years. Many women experience the constant challenge of finding PPE (Personal Protective Equipment) uniforms that fit the curves of a woman's body. Personally I've found it difficult to find safety glasses that fit a smaller female face, which means dealing with dust and grit flying in from the sides. Gloves can also be an issue, with most being too large for some smaller women's hands. Only recently has the emergence of women specific PPE, namely shirts, pants and boots, made an appearance on the market, and eventually into larger organisations. Businesses like *She's Empowered*, *She Wear Australia* and *Eve Workwear* have recognised the need for women to be clothed in comfortable, well-fitting clothes to enable them to work safely, productively and confidently. I strongly suggest that if your organisation doesn't already offer female PPE items, give the above companies a call to see what they have on offer.

Being disrespected, condescended and treated differently to the men

When the most common phrase referring to someone at work is "mate" it can feel very condescending to be referred to as "love" or "good girl". I once mentioned this to a male manager after witnessing one of his female staff subtly cringe after he called her "love". He was shocked, he never meant anything negative by it, and after all, it was a term of endearment and habit, not personal. But what he didn't realise is that he called the rest of his male team "mate". This differentiation was alienating to the woman and made her feel as though she was different to the rest of the team. Other women have experienced similar feelings of differentiation and even disrespect. When women were asked whether they felt they were treated equally to the men at work 26% said yes, 35% said no and the remaining 39% felt the respect was conditional. One project and design engineer said "I always question this. It is not too bad on the surface but I hear rumours of comments behind closed doors and I then I realise there is still a long way to go". Whilst an Executive Assistant in Construction said: "I'm in a 'female role' so I think this determines how 'equal' I am". On the other hand, the women who did feel they were treated equally recognised that in some situations, women get treated better than the men; "yes sometimes even better even though that's not quite fair". Another woman who has worked across agriculture and mining stated that "most men these days are respectful and excited for a woman to come on board". However out of those women who felt disrespected there was a theme of being undervalued in their job; "they (men) can be rather degrading about your abilities physically" said a rail operator. Whilst an electrical apprentice felt "They (men) judge them (women) a lot more harsh.

Women have a lot more to prove to men in the workplace especially in leadership roles. It takes ages to build credibility and not long for it to be destroyed".

Social expectations of child care and having babies

This undoubtedly affects woman across all industries, not just the masculine ones. Research shows that women still shoulder the brunt of household duties and child-minding responsibilities, even when they work full time (Australian Institute of Families Studies, 2013). It was found that full-time working mothers, who have a child under five years of age, undertake 3.6 hours of child care and 2.4 hours of housework each day. Compare this to the 2.6 hours of childcare and 1.8 hours of housework per day completed by fathers when the mother works full time.

If these statistics hold true for women working in the masculine industries then they can present significant challenges. The work days in most masculine industries can be long, sometimes inflexible and often remotely based. This makes it difficult for a woman to juggle the demands of her job with the social expectations of her role as primary carer. But it's not impossible! It takes the acceptance and understanding of her manager/employer to provide flexible working options (i.e. working from home, working on a weekend, etc.) and most importantly, for men to start taking on an equal share of home and child duties. This second suggestion is one that jabs at the culture of our industry. Many of the men in leadership positions have a partner who stays at home to manage the running of the household. This arrangement could be for a variety of reasons; she enjoys being a stay-at-home mother, she can't find work in their area, or her partner earns enough to live on the one income. However, with this arrangement there is also the risk of reinforcing the unconscious biases that the role of a woman is at home and not in the workforce. This same bias means it is strange, ridiculous or simply unacceptable for a working man to be worrying about child care and house duties. In the broader society and in more progressive industries people are working to try to break this stereotype. However, it may take the masculine industries a little longer than most to shift. I have seen young managers get irritated by the women in their team who request carer's leave for sick children, or who leave early to make the school pick up. I've even had a Director (probably aged in his late 50s) of a construction company tell me (in front of eight other female graduates) that if women found the industry so difficult, maybe they shouldn't work here. However, on the flip side of this, I have also seen General Managers arrive at work after dropping their kids at school and supervisors grant their male team members an early leave to catch their kid's baseball game. An engineer once told me a story she had witnessed at work where a female site engineer with a three-year-old daughter fought for six months to work four days a week. She spoke with two Project Managers who both said no. She then changed jobs and began working for another Project Manager who said yes and set about making the flexible work possible. It is interesting to notice that this Project Manager also had children and a wife who worked. Of the two PMs who said no, one didn't have kids and the other had a wife who did not work. So whilst things are changing, they are changing slowly, and appear intrinsically tied to each person's experience, rather than a cultural acceptance.

There is also the ever-present question mark that dangles over the head of every young woman, especially if she's in a serious relationship: when is she going to get pregnant? For some workplaces, particularly those that are office based and located in metropolitan areas, a pregnant woman might not pose too many challenges. She works up to the start of her maternity leave, goes away, has the baby, probably drops in to see the team a few weeks later with baby in tow, gets invited to team events and may even decide to re-commence working on a part-time basis with the vision of returning to full-time down the track. However, for women working in remote locations pregnancy can present other challenges. On some FIFO sites, pregnant women must leave work well before the start of their maternity leave due to restrictions on flying. Some remote townships won't allow pregnant women to stay in the town due to insufficient medical resources to deal with birthing complications. I've also heard of companies struggling to cover the maternity leave, particularly in the pink ghetto roles (heavily populated by females), when a number of team members become pregnant around the same time. These challenges associated with women getting pregnant and having babies can seem like an inconvenience to an industry that historically never had to deal with such matters.

Having your appearance scrutinised and commented on

A young female engineer once told me she hated going out to construction sites because it meant she had to wear PPE pants. When I asked her what was the matter with the pants she said she'd had comments made about the shape and size of her bottom and felt mortally embarrassed each time she had to wear them. It was obvious to see from talking to this young woman how much this was affecting her self-esteem and ultimately her comfort in her job. Unfortunately, this type of intimidating and harassing behaviour is indicative of a society that feels it can pass judgement on a woman's body and the actions she chooses to do with it. Just turn on the TV, or walk through the magazine aisle and it's hard to ignore the judgement and scrutiny women are put under. However, when it's in our workplace and directed at us, it is personal and very uncomfortable. When you are the only one having your appearance commented on, it can make you feel isolated and separate from the group. Many women will try to downplay their female appearance in an attempt to blend in. An electrical apprentice commented that "I wear boy's pants at work for that reason. They're baggier and don't hug my figure as much. I ensure my shorts and exercise pants on site are past my knees to try and avoid unwanted attention." This downplaying of the feminine appearance is something a lot of women are conscious of, across all levels of an organisation, from Project Managers to administration staff. A project coordinator in the construction industry said: "I can't even walk into the office with my hair straightened or my nails painted without someone making a passing remark – usually in good fun but they pick up on these things and it bothers me." It's this constant attention that can make the working environment uncomfortable. Early in my career, I found this attention frustrating and difficult to manage. I too would downplay my feminine appearance as much as possible by wearing

73

baggy male uniforms, keeping my hair in a low tight bun, wearing no makeup, nail polish or jewellery. However, the men would still notice and make comment about any little change to this initial image. One day I wore a purple sweater to work, only to have the site Superintendent walk past me with a bunch of blokes and make a comment about how it showed my curves. I never wore that sweater to work again. On other occasions comments have simply come from painting my nails a different colour, changing a hairstyle or wearing particular earings. They weren't rude comments, but simply having your appearance commented on, when no one else's appearance is being critiqued is uncomfortable. When all you're trying to do is be accepted for your work and your performance, comments about insignificant things like your appearance are frustrating. It devalues your capabilities and purpose for being on site. This constant process of second-guessing your appearance and downplaying personal preferences to avoid comments and trying to blend in is stressful and mentally taxing.

Having your abilities doubted

There is an old quote by Charlotte Whitton (a former Mayor of Ottawa) which goes "Whatever women do they must do twice as well as men to be thought half as good. Luckily, this is not difficult." This quote resonates strongly with many women in the masculine industries who have felt their ability, strength and intelligence questioned. A project geologist in the mining industry iterated the words of Charlotte Whitton when she stated that "a female will often have to prove that she knows what she is talking about or that she can physically do the work before getting the respect of the guys, she often needs to be better than they are and needs to make sure they will not walk over her because they will try." The tricky thing about being a minority is that you stand out from the norm. All your actions and behaviours are amplified because they are coming from a place of difference. This feeling of having to prove yourself can be stressful, particularly when you're new and unknown to a site or a team. In this situation, the only thing people have to go on is the role you occupy and the fact that you're a female. The role you hold will have its own stereotypes associated with it, for instance we all have stereotypes of an engineer or a human resource advisor, and being a female carries obvious stereotypes of its own. Often people use these stereotypes to form their judgement of someone who they don't know. After all, it's easier for the brain to process if it can liken you to something already familiar. However, this does not mean the stereotypical judgement is correct and this is what many women must overcome in the masculine industries. A field engineer in the oil and gas industry expressed frustration at the men "assuming I can't OR shouldn't have to do something physically because I'm a girl, resulting in dudes trying to run roughshod over what I'm doing." Other women have relayed the experiences of being talked over in meetings, not being allowed to operate certain equipment and having their suggestions rejected by the team/manager only to have them presented by a man as his own later on. Whilst these situations are demoralising, they can also have a motivating effect to spur women on to prove their worth. In fact, I have seen this to be the case more often than not! I once worked with a female underground worker who was known in her crew to be able to shotcrete a wall (i.e. spray a concrete-like substance onto a surface) better than any other man. I have seen female Supervisors muck in and do the dirtiest of jobs (when another male Supervisor wouldn't)

75

just to prove she's as good as any of the blokes on her crew. I've even been known to throw around 20kg bags of cement mix just to prove that women can be strong too! Fortunately, in this day and age most organisations have restrictions on the weights you're allowed to lift and the method in which manual handling is to be conducted. As one tradesperson remarked, "there is technology to overcome it! Nobody wants to wear out their body, men or women". Yet, the reality is that a smaller female body may not be able to lift the same weight as a muscular man and this can be "a bit degrading, like admitting you don't belong" (Field Engineer). Therefore, not only do you have to contend with others doubting your abilities, your own nagging self-doubts are never far behind.

Of course, this list of challenges is not exhaustive. There are other challenges, such as being paid less, dealing with aggression and dominance, and feeling lonely, which are experienced by women in masculine industries. Rather than discuss these themes briefly here, I will explore them (and others) throughout the different chapters of the book.

It is also important to recognise that whilst I have discussed the above challenges as being specific to women, they are not exclusively experienced by women. Some men may also experience a range of these challenges through their own experiences of working in the masculine industries. There will be some men who feel comfortable with the feminine and hence experience the masculine industry in ways similar to many females. We must also remember that not all females will experience the masculine industries in the way described in this chapter because they may feel comfortable engaging in and demonstrating masculine behaviour. Neither situation is better or worse than the other. The most important takeaway from all of this is the understanding that if we truly want diversity in our masculine industries we need to be aware of the challenges that exist for people who are "diverse" from the current norm. It is not to blame, or cast judgement, but rather to understand the reality of our current situation so that we can make better decisions for the future which we are building.

PART 3

Men's Business

"The male has paid a heavy price for his masculine 'privilege' and power. He is out of touch with his emotions and his body. He is playing by the rules of the male game plan and with lemming-like purpose he is destroying himself — emotionally, psychologically and physically."

Herb Goldberg

It's a Man's World

A female mentor of mine once told me off for using the phrase "male dominant" when describing the work environment of construction and mining. She suggested we should instead call it "male prevalent". Her rationale was that whilst the majority of employees in these industries are men, it does not necessarily mean men are dominant. I initially agreed that "male dominant" never sat well with me but her alternative phrase "male prevalent" didn't hit the mark either. I felt as though on the average, men did have the upper hand in our workplaces and the description of "male prevalent" underplayed the culture which I and many other women were operating in.

This culture I allude to is one best described as aggressive, sometimes violent, driven by fear, competition and containing big egos. In other words, it's a highly masculine culture. This environment is more than just "male prevalent", it is deeper than physicality and biology. This is a culture, deeply rooted in values, norms and behaviours.

My preference is to describe the industries which consist primarily of men as "masculine workplaces". Typically, the work environments of masculine workplaces include political game playing, aggressiveness, backstabbing, point-scoring, overconfidence and 'stitching people up' (Davey 2008).

I have always wondered whether this was just my female perspective on the culture of the masculine industries, but on speaking to men it turns out they have a similar perspective.

A long time mining and construction worker described these industries as "the only macho businesses left". On further inquiry as to what he meant by "macho", he explained that it's an opinionated culture, where "most people have a false sense of their balls being too big". To counter this he did describe the industries "can-do" attitude of achieving a lot with very little. This resourcefulness he attributed to the industries staying power and ability to ride the booms and busts.

A younger male perspective was sought from an engineer in a major construction company. He explained his industry like "a big playground", where there are "characters similar to school". On inquiry as to what this meant he explained that in construction you've got the big personalities, the ones who want to "conquer the world". He explained these conquering types can be either nice guys, or real assholes, depending on their personality. When questioned about his feelings towards construction he loved the challenge and variety of work the industry throws his way. When I asked what his favourite thing about construction was he eagerly replied: "not being inside all day"! The downside he discussed was the seriousness of his role's responsibilities. As an engineer, he is required to sign off compliance documents and as he said: "if shit goes downhill, your name's on everything". When queried about the interactions between guys on site, the young engineer confirmed humour, competition and dominance to be daily factors in the masculine industry.

An excellent account of the masculinity of the mining industry is discussed in Dean Laplonge's book So You Think You're Tough? Getting serious about gender in mining. In this book, Laplonge explores the masculine culture within the mining industry. He does not use the phrase "male dominant", rather he uses terms such as masculine and feminine to describe culture, which I support completely. His rationale for taking this approach is rooted in the reality that not every man is like "all men" and not every woman is like "all women". Within the genders, there is variety in how individuals express both masculine and feminine characteristics (i.e. the gender spectrum).

Laplonge explores how masculinity is practised in the mining industry. He states that through his research he has found a culturally expected way in which men on a mine site are "allowed" to act. This culture is not formed purely because there are more men present; it arises from the group's allowance of a particular kind of masculinity being expressed by group members. Our society has come up with a variety of terms to describe a range of different masculine behaviours; S.N.A.G's, metrosexuals, bikies, bogans, hipsters and more. Each of these descriptions conjures up an image and the behaviours of the man who fits into each group.

Laplonge's book explores the type of masculinity which is endemic in the mining industry, and which he says is practised by both men and women in this industry. This includes:

- Working long hours
- Coping on your own and not requiring support from others
- Physical strength and force used to get the job done
- Getting dirty
- Using work systems to control and dominate
- Achieving high levels of production to signify masculinity

81

He is right on the money when it comes to describing the culture of not only mining, but of other masculine industries, such as construction. To put it in to context, let me provide you with real life examples of how the masculinity described by Laplonge gets played out in real life.

Working long hours.

Typically the work day will consist of 12-14+ hours for many sequential days or even weeks at a time. Rosters do vary across different sites, projects or organisations but the standard 12-hour day tends to remain consistent. I've worked with men who will, without fail be the first one to work each day (unless he's deathly ill). They will also be one of the last to leave at the end of the day. I even found myself subscribing to the same ideology of arriving early and leaving late to make a good impression on my colleagues. There is real value placed on face-time, rather than efficient time, in the masculine industries.

Coping on your own and not requiring support from others.

The common saying of "real men don't cry" is no truer than in a masculine industry. As a workplace coach I have been privileged to work with a range of leaders, mainly men. What I have noticed is that in some of the more hyper-masculine places I've worked, men seem disinterested and degrading of the role of coach. It is seen as fluffy and unnecessary. Seeking help, particularly for emotional or personal matters is rare in the masculine industries, and if done at all it is gone about quietly and secretively.

Physical strength and force used get the job done.

Physical strength is generally well regarded in most masculine industries. I've noticed that large men tend to have better presence and tend to be listened to more than when a smaller man is speaking. This is particularly evident in group communications. However, in some roles strength and size is a real benefit to completing the job. When I was working in an underground mine a Shift Supervisor and I headed to a crib room to collect paperwork. When we entered the crib room (which was really just an alcove dug out of the dirt wall with a few tables and chairs thrown in) I found it to be full of proteins, supplement powders and magazines scattered about. My initial thought was "here we go… looks like I've found their stash of pornos", but when I looked closer the magazines were actually dedicated to male fitness and body building. I was surprised as the crib shed magazines I'd seen on other sites were usually of the big busted lady types. Yet these magazines indicated a different culture of this particular crew who used the crib room. It turned out these blokes were big units, with large biceps and wide chests, and were responsible for some of the more physically intensive jobs in the underground and took pride in their physical size and strength.

Getting dirty.

Getting dirty tends to be a common occurrence in the masculine industries, particularly if your role is based on a site. Usually the work is outside and involves digging dirt, shifting minerals, grease, oils, concrete, paint, dust, rain, chemicals, and the list goes on. Getting grubby tends to be a badge of honour. It signifies you've done a "good day's work", gotten in there and made it happen. I've known men to deliberately scuff up their new steel cap boots so they look worn in, and I've seen blokes get the mickey taken out of them for wearing a bright new PPE shirt to work. When you look grubby, the implied message is that you know what's really happening on the job, and that you're not just some "shiny ass" who sits in his/her air-conditioned office all day. On a personal note, getting dirty is one of my favourite things about working in a masculine industry. I love that I can spill something on myself and no one bats an eyelid because it's usually mixed in there with dirt, grease and whatever mineral we're digging out of the ground.

Using work systems to control and dominate.

Many masculine industries are dangerous. There are serious risks that if not managed correctly could result in major injury or death. Therefore, systems are an important part of managing this risk. However, when taken to the extreme some systems and processes can also stifle the creativity and innovation in many larger masculine organisations. In the recent downturn experienced by the resource industries many organisations have gone bust, partly due to their inability to respond quickly to their changed environment. Others

84

have taken the initiative to review their processes and procedures in search of more efficient ways of operating. This has involved seeking suggestions and ideas from people at all levels of the business on ways to improve efficiency, reduce waste, and save dollars. It will be interesting to see how this new behaviour of innovation continues to evolve in the masculine industries.

Achieving high levels of production to signify masculinity.

Productivity targets are gospel in any mining organisation. This is the information you want to know when you step on to any mine site: what tonnes are they chasing, is it higher or lower than last year, how are they tracking towards achieving this? Same goes for a construction site: what's the budget, when does the job need to be completed, are they on schedule? Productivity is so important that I have seen people sacrifice themselves and others to achieve it. They will strive for productivity at all costs, just to save face and to not look like they let the team down. However, chasing high production targets can sometimes lead to negative outcomes: people cut corners, neglect safety, rush jobs, compromise quality and leave a mess for their team mates to clean up just so they themselves look good. This ties in with the discussion that a masculine perspective tends to be more achievement orientated, whereas a feminine perspective looks more at the process of achieving the goal.

The above descriptions go a little way into painting the picture of what it's like to work in a masculine environment. In the following sections we will explore at greater depth some of the other situations you may encounter whilst working in a masculine workplace.

The Pecking Order

There is a lot of discussion surrounding the group dynamics of men, particularly men who are orientated towards the masculine end of the spectrum.

A masculine group is one that is structured with a hierarchy, or in other words, a pecking order. There is generally an alpha, then a select few close allies and nearly all the rest will be followers who slot themselves in along the hierarchy. They will jostle, tease and challenge one another to see who gets to be above whom, or in other words, who is standing on which rung.

Another interesting thing seems to occur in the male group dynamics and that's the position of the outlier. This is a person who may be the joker of the group, the class clown, the one who the other guys don't particularly like much, but who allow his membership to the group because he serves a purpose. This purpose could be for amusement, because he does hilarious things, or pushes the boundary of appropriateness where the others won't go, but wish they could. Or his membership could be safe due to his connections or relationship with other important people either internal or external to the group. An alternative theory is that he is kept in the group as an assurance to the other group members that the bottom rung of the hierarchical ladder is occupied by someone other than themselves. It is a strategy of self-preservation to ensure they don't end up at the bottom of the hierarchy.

This type of behaviour can be witnessed in groups of men, young and old. At school, it was evident with the teenage boys, who would hang around in a large group. There was the alpha boy, who dictated what was cool, and the other boys fell into line. Rarely was this alpha challenged. It was more common to see challenges amongst his closest allies who would jostle one another in an attempt to be his right-hand man.

At work things get a little more complicated where we have to factor in the formal hierarchy of organisational positions. Generally, the boss will be respected, not necessarily because of any personal characteristics, but because of the position he occupies. A masculine brain will respect the chain of command. That is, unless he is a hyper-masculine alpha male who thinks the boss above him is a goose. If this is the case, don't be surprised if you see him challenge his boss. This challenge may be in a direct form, or it could be more covert by undermining him in front of someone even higher up the hierarchy. This tactic is about "one-upping" the boss to make the alpha look better.

When we start to look at male group dynamics without the formal organisational hierarchy, we tend to see a model more resemblant of the schoolyard. This is because all group members are formally at the same level. An example of how this plays out at work can be observed in a mining or construction crew (excluding the supervisor). In these groups, there is very little formal differentiation and most people are employed on roughly the same level. However, you will still see an expression of hierarchy if the group has more than eight members. Sometimes the hierarchy will emerge due to the nature of the trade skills possessed by people. Each trade is very protective of their skills and likes to be derogatory towards the other trades. For example, electricians have the reputation of thinking they're the intelligent trade, whereas other trades tease them for being soft and afraid to get their hands dirty. Other factors which can determine hierarchy are experience levels, union membership, relationships with key people, physical size, culture, gender and personality.

An example of how male dynamics play out in a work team was explained to me by a male construction site engineer. He recounted a story about receiving an aggressive email from a bullish peer which questioned the quality of his work. Normally these types of emails would not ruffle him but it was the fact that the bullish peer had cc'd in numerous senior managers and was questioning his integrity in front of important people. In other words, the peer was trying to one-up him in front of those who could influence their career success. As you can imagine, he was pissed off. So his tactic was to "reply all" (to his peer and the managers) with a response that set the record straight and kept his reputation intact. The response was exactly as he had hoped. The peer sent back a brief email, without cc'ing to anyone else, and apologised for drawing the wrong conclusions. The dynamics between these two men has now changed in such a way that the very same peer is now more likely to pick up the phone to speak to my engineer friend, rather than send another abusive email.

In this scenario, my friend used the right tactics for dealing with an aggressive peer. He set a standard by responding in a calm, objective fashion which clearly outlined the facts and didn't buy into any emotions. Yet, that very simple email sent a message to the group that he would not put up with someone responding aggressively to him, nor would he respond in a similarly emotional way. The last thing we want to do is engage in a back-and-forth email debate where each party is trying to undermine the other, especially not in front of our managers.

If the bullish peer had decided to stick to his guns and continue to attack the engineer via another public email my recommendation would be to respond one final time, with everyone cc'd in, and suggest that since the matter isn't being resolved over email it's best to speak face to face (as first preference) or over the phone. This sends a clear message that you're standing resolute and won't be intimidated, but that you're taking the lead to resolve the issue whilst not wasting the time (and filling up the inbox) of the managers.

The game of bonding

Relationship building between men is no different than between women. It's all about finding something in common that you can talk about, share an interest in and hopefully avoid any awkward silences. However, the difference comes when we start to look at what we relate about and how we relate to one another.

Let me share with you a story. It was quite early in my career when I joined a major construction project. Prior to this role I had worked at a couple of different mine sites and was feeling pretty comfortable with the masculine environment I was about to step in to. The role I took on was to report directly to the HR Manager who was a well-respected professional, not only in his own company but across the industry. I was excited to work with him and to learn from his experience.

In the first few weeks of my job I made an effort to visit all of the managers and as many of the Superintendents as I could. I was on a mission to build relationships. At one of my fortnightly catch-ups with my manager he asked how I was going in this space. I explained that it was a mixed response. Some were welcoming, supportive and offered their assistance where necessary. Others were friendly but still very distant and the remaining group were cold, disinterested and aloof. We discussed my approach with each different person and how I could tailor my style to be more like theirs when I was communicating. My manager then suggested that in order to find common ground with the men I should learn a thing or two about rugby.

What?! I was affronted.

Not only did his suggestion offend me by implying that I didn't know anything about sports (I'd been raised on the stuff thank you very much) but that I was expected to learn about the game *they* found most interesting. Nothing was said about the fact we were working in an AFL state, and AFL was the game I knew about, so why didn't *they* learn about the game I knew. Coupled with that I was pissed off that my work relationships were somehow tied up with how much I knew about a non-work related thing like sport. Of course, I didn't say anything about my thoughts to my manager. How could I? I felt it would be a dead end conversation where I would wind up sounding like a whinger. Instead I thanked him for the advice and went on my (not so) merry way.

On reflection I realised his advice may have been valuable. Once I got over my little self-righteous huff, I began to realise how useful it was. In fact, it turns out to be a tactic used by other women to build relationships with the men in their workplace.

Sally, a young project manager in a construction company agrees it's an excellent way to build relationships. "It definitely helps build relationships but I would never expect the guys to discuss last night's episode of The Bachelor with me… (but)… footy and cricket I'm on top of but always find myself bluffing my way through NBA and soccer conversations – which results in frantic Googling".

However it turns out that in some workplaces, the blokes are quite happy to discuss the latest happenings on reality TV. Jess, a HR professional works in a company just like this. "I like in our workplace we have conversations about all sorts of topics. The guys are usually more up with the latest reality series than I am, and my male boss calls me for advice about bikes! It can be hard though when the various world cups are on – I usually try to steer the conversation towards something more mutually interesting – if you talk to someone for long enough you'll always find something in common!"

Finding something in common seems to be the key for any relationship. Emma, a machinery operator found that discussions of sport led to discovering other similar interests, "My Sons were very involved in footy and quite good at it. Working in a male dominated work place, this definitely helped. It initiated many conversations on footy all round. I of course was happy to talk about my sons' footy. I noticed the guys like talking about their families".

So while sport is not necessarily the only topic of interest in a masculine workplace it seems to be a pretty safe topic to raise if you want to win some brownie points. Yet, I'm not going to be so arrogant as to suggest that every man is interested in sport, you just need to keep your ears tuned in to pick up the major topics of conversation. If you're not sure of the topics of interest, or you're new to the masculine group, you could test the water with a little sport themed comment. After all, the prevalence of golf days, footy matches, and fishing trips which get arranged amongst workmates suggests to me that sport and recreation is a fairly safe topic to start with.

Now I can imagine many of you are thinking: "Why should I be the one to learn about something new, why can't the boys learn what I'm interested in"? Or maybe it was just me thinking that. Anyway, the thought crossed my mind and was something I had grappled with. I realised that my options were twofold; I could choose to remain disinterested, which would probably result in being left out of conversations or events, or I could spend a couple of hours brushing up on a sport.

I've decided that personally, the latter is my best option. My job is all about relationships, and building rapport with people is of the utmost importance. Therefore, sometimes you've got to go outside your own comfort zone in the interest of building commonality. The rules are the same for either gender; it makes no difference whether you're trying to connect with a man or a woman. Find something in common, and if that fails (and the relationship is important to you) expect to do some quick Googling! Who knows, you might end up liking what you learn.

So now we've covered the "what" to talk about (i.e. find something in common), now we need to discuss the "how".

Getting the Last Laugh

For anyone who's spent time around all male groups, it becomes quite obvious that humour plays a big part in their bonding processes. Humour is used to confirm our views of the world; it can signify the norms, values and conflicts of a group. It is suggested that humour is used as a way of defining hierarchies, particularly when the butt of a joke is at the expense of a group to which we don't belong. This is particularly evident in the male group dynamics where we see one individual receive the majority of teasing, or when a group of carpenters take-the-piss out of the electricians. On the flip side of this is the use of humour to build relationships. This can be to create bonds with other people or to reduce stress and tension through a shared joke.

A few years ago I was coaching a Supervisor called John. John had spent many years in the military and had done a number of different tours overseas. He had experienced some pretty harrowing situations which had inevitably influenced his perspective on the world. During our coaching time together he shared his concern about the relationship he had with his crew. John was worried that he wasn't really connecting with his crew and at times felt they didn't really like him. After speaking to some of John's crew members as well as his Superintendent it came to light that John was regarded as a bit of a stiff. The guys thought he was arrogant and his Superintendent wished he would lighten up a bit. John and I discussed a number of different strategies, which focused on the physical (i.e. body language) and the verbal interactions (i.e. how and what he spoke about) and realised that what was missing from John's interactions with the crew was a bit of humour. John made a commitment to try out a few more jokes with the crew, and over time found that the connection between them slowly grew.

As a whole, it has been found that compared to women, men use humour more regularly and that their jokes tend to be perceived as funnier (by both men and women strangely enough). It may also come as no surprise that the major topics of jokes amongst men have been found to involve hostile and sexual content.

However, something different happens when we start to look at groups of either all male or all female. What we find is that in groups of all female, there is actually more joking and laughing than in all-male groups. Whilst the research is not definitive as to why, I'm going to go out on a limb to suggest that in all-female groups humour is often used to build connections amongst group members, rather than as a tool to establish hierarchy. In my experience, when I'm in an all-woman group I am much more aware of building egalitarian relationships with my fellow ladies. However, when I'm in an all-male group (and I'm the only woman) I feel much more ready for the jokes which may challenge me, or where I can throw a humorous challenge out to someone else. Something I would be unlikely to do amongst my girlfriends.

However with a vast majority of men working in very masculine environments, this challenging humour is something which is evident. An example of this occurred when I was working in the underground. I was new to this site, and to make matters worse, was only 1 of 3 other women who would head down below surface with the men. Needless to say, the guys were not used to having a woman in the drifty (the car which transports people underground). The first few times with each crew was uncomfortable; the boys were quiet, they'd barely make eye contact with me and for some odd reason I always had plenty of space around me in an otherwise chocker-block cabin – I think they were afraid of catching my girl germs. But after a little while with the same crew, after they got to know me and realised I was easy going they began to open up. They started the talk to me, would throw banter around the crew and then one day something amazing happened that let me know I had finally been accepted … I became the butt of one their jokes. I forget now exactly how they teased me, but it was light-hearted and completely inoffensive. Yet it was in that moment, with that small gesture, I realised I was in! I had been accepted into the crew.

The thing with a lot of environments in the masculine industry is that they are tough; dirty, dusty, muddy, noisy, smelly, cramped. Humour is a great way of making light of what you're dealing with and to ease the tension and stress that a harsh environment can cause. However, like most things in life you need a balance and it's important to realise when the humour goes too far.

Whilst nearly everyone appreciates a joke, it can often be a fine line between something funny, and something offensive. The challenge in the industry over the past decade is how to tame this humour in a way that still provides the benefits of bonding and stress reduction, without causing offense or anxiety to anyone else.

Let me tell you a tale from the old days to explain what I mean.

Picture this … it's a freezing cold morning out on a mine site. Everyone is feeling pretty miserable and gloomy due to the weather. The Leading Hand of the crew decides something needs to be done to lighten the mood. He goes outside, drops his dacks, positions his butt over a shovel and lays out a nice fresh steamy poop. The Leading Hand picks up the shovel, marches back inside and places the still steaming surprise on the crib room table with the question, "do you guys reckon I'm getting enough fiber"? The crew is immediately thrown into an uproar. Blokes start yelling "get the fuck out of here you dirty bastard!" One bloke vomits into his crib box and the others start scrambling away from the table. The Leading Hand chuckles and feels pretty pleased with himself, at least now the crew is alive and energised.

Here's another story for you. A bloke was climbing onto the coal dredger (which is a large multistorey machine designed to dig up coal from the ground). His workmate was in the cabin above and had just discovered a brown rotten pear which had been left by a previous crew. This guy thought it would be excellently funny to drop the pear over the edge and immediately stick his bare bum over the railing. The dropped pear hits the guy walking up the dredger on the shoulder. He looks down and sees brown rotten gloop down his shirt and looks up to see a bare arse hanging over the edge. It doesn't take a genius to realise the poor bloke thinks he's just been shat on. "I'm gonna fucking kill you" he screams to the other guy and races up to sort the other bloke out. The funny thing is, once he realised it was only a pear he was sweet. They laughed like old chums about it and shared the story with the rest of the blokes over some post-work beers.

There are millions of stories just like this which were daily occurrences in the by-gone era of the masculine workplace. However now, if the same scenario played out, it is very likely the jokesters would be performance managed or even terminated. In today's world companies will not and cannot tolerate humour which degrades another. Legally, they are liable to provide a workplace which is safe, physically and psychologically, for everyone. Therefore, many of the blokes who started their career in the "good ol' days" have had to learn to curb their humour. This has been difficult for some of them.

When you get to talking with some of the older workers, Supervisors, Superintendents and even some Managers there is a wistfulness for the old days. Some of them are even downright angry they can't get away with the same shenanigans, and some blame the introduction of women into the industry for this shift; as one of them once told me "no offense love, but before you women came along we could get away with a lot more".

That Winning Feeling

The competition amongst males sure gets a fair bit of airplay. From seeing who can "score" the hot chick at the bar, to landing the promotion at work, many males revel in the opportunity to outdo one another.

It comes as no surprise that in masculine workplaces we tend to find these competitive types. They're pretty hard to miss actually. Generally energetic, assertive, sometimes aggressive, they do their best to stand out from the crowd. These are the alpha-males, the ones breaking targets, hitting the tonnes and slashing the budget at work. Sometimes they're also the ones buying the fancy cars, nice watches and expensive toys – reminders to everyone else around them that this alpha-male is totally winning at life.

97

However, not every bloke is that extreme, and nor is it only blokes who enjoy competition. Some women, including yours truly, love a bit of healthy competition. It's what keeps me going, spurs me on – the drive that helps me overcome any self-doubts that creep in. The drive of competition is therefore not owned solely by the male gender, but it does seem to feature more heavily in their behaviours.

When it comes to the research it does appear men outdo women in the competitiveness stakes. In fact, they're probably high-fiving one another for winning that one. It also appears that the difference in competitiveness between the genders starts at an early age.

An interesting experiment asked a group of nine and ten-year-old kids to run around a track whilst being timed. They found that when there was no competition, the girls and boys completed the task at basically the same time (at that age there is little to no physical difference in running ability). However, when the kids were put into competition with one another, the boys' times improved whereas the girls' times didn't change. It was as if the competition had no effect on the girls. This result had the researchers questioning the effect of gender differences towards physical activity and gender stereotyping.

This competitive split between the genders doesn't get any better as we age. Even in adults, we find that Western men are more competitive than Western women. However, in societies with matrilineal structures (where ancestry is traced through the female lines, not the male's line like our western society) it's actually the opposite, women are more competitive. This suggests that nurture (i.e. social influences) can actually change how competitive someone becomes. But let's not leave biology out because

98

apparently, the time of the month and whether we're on a certain type of contraception can also influence how competitive we feel.

Irrespective of all this, it begs to reason that our blokes working in the Western masculine industries of Australia will have an average level of competitiveness higher than the average female population. And boy does this play out at work!

Take the story of a young site engineer named Ted. Normally Ted is a pretty cool customer. He's got good self-awareness, understands the macho games, and is a pretty decent guy all round. This particular day on site it was stinking hot and Ted was out with a crew giving instructions on how to dig a trench. Unfortunately, the crew's digging techniques were not to Ted's liking, and Ted's directions were not to the crew's liking either. So a fairly heated conversation ensued. The banter went back and forth, each challenging the other on the best way to dig the trench and each wanting to win the argument. It got to the point where Ted was so worked up he broke protocol by jumping in the trench to begin digging like a mad-man in the sun, just to prove his way was best. I wonder which of the men actually thought they had won the argument: the guy digging the hole in the sun, or the ones watching him dig.

These moments of enhanced competitiveness are said to be related to a rise in cortisol levels. In men who tend to have an "everyday" drive for status, they will also experience a surge of testosterone. This became evident to me whilst working on a highly adversarial construction site that was dealing with a range of industrial issues, time delays and budget concerns. Needless to say, the environment was tense and competition was rife. The Industrial Relations team and the Union delegates would have meetings which often turned into fist-pounding, yelling matches. Both sides wanted to conquer the other (just like in the hierarchy chapter) and neither side wanted to "lose". Throughout the many meetings, I often wondered just how much of the "discussion" was productive and how much of it was actually hot air with some chest-thumping thrown in. After all, situations that cause us to be under stress can impair our performance and decision-making abilities.

Yet not all male competition in the industry results in such large displays of competitiveness. There are many more light-hearted versions that incorporate humour which gets played out during the course of a day. If you spend time amongst a crew you will soon learn about the "carton" deal. In the event that a team member stuffs up, breaks something or forgets something, they will be penalised and required to purchase "a carton" (usually of beer) to share with the rest of the crew. We all know that if you hear the words "Ah… that's a carton mate", you better turn up with a slab of beer at the next team barbie, or else you'll be getting the burnt sausages!

Competition across most masculine industries is rife, from the footy tipping and lunchtime gambling to the more audacious production and utilisation rates, the masculine guys are gunning for top position. This eagerness to compete and ultimately win can have a negative effect when a more feminine person comes into the equation. A number of years ago I was asked to coach Jeff, a middle-aged Supervisor. Jeff was a big bloke, tall and broad, his presence was immediately felt when he entered the room or walked amongst the crew. This dude was a great example of the masculine man. The crew, consisting of mainly men and 1 masculine female, seemed to have a healthy respect for him. When I asked why, their immediate response was "because he gets shit done". Jeff was known on site for pushing the crew to get tonnes (as long as it was safe) and was always trying to outdo previous records. The day before Jeff and I were due to meet, he and his crew had broken the long-standing production record for that site. When Jeff and I met the next morning this was one of the very first things he told me. This eager self-promotion was but another hint that I was dealing with a very masculine bloke. Jeff was proud, not so much about the efforts of the crew, but that he knew how to drive them to get production! The focus for Jeff was not on the "we" it was on the "me", a perspective more commonly attributed to masculine individuals.

The contrast of this was observed in Jeff's peer, and alternative Supervisor, Sally (who was also another of my coachees). Sally did possess some masculine traits of her own but her feminine side was more prominent. Particularly when compared to Jeff's masculine style. When I mentioned the record that Jeff broke, she scoffed and rolled her eyes. When I dug a little further into her response she explained that it was all well and good that Jeff had broken the record, but he'd left the work area in a complete mess and had not set up for the oncoming shift. Sally did not share the enjoyment or drive of breaking the record when all the other responsibilities had been abandoned in pursuit of the record tonnes. Whilst they managed to get great productivity for the business in that one 12 hour shift, they had actually created more work for the oncoming crew which caused that crew to have low productivity.

This difference in perspective is a good example of the competitive differences between masculine and feminine individuals. Jeff was focused on breaking the record (i.e. the end result); whereas Sally was worried about the other factors affected by this win (i.e. the mess he'd left for the oncoming crew and the way he had run the plant).

It is interesting to know that men are more likely to apply for jobs in competitive environments. This makes me wonder… as we get more women into trades and engineering roles (i.e. we begin feeding the pipeline with women), it stands to reason that we will eventually get more women Supervisors, Superintendents and Managers. However, if our masculine industries remain the hyper-competitive environments they are, potentially many women (assuming these women are more feminine than masculine) entering the pipeline may lose interest in "competing" for the top jobs. I've started to get an inkling this may be a frightening reality already. I've come across a number of young women, who are early in their careers, and they have no interest in becoming a leader of people. When I ask them why the response is often "I don't know. I just can't see myself doing that".

Why?!

Why don't you see yourself doing that? You're smart, savvy and capable (and I've seen you hold your ground out in the field, or in a managers' meeting). What is holding you back from competing for that vacant job higher up the organisational hierarchy?

The answer could actually lie in the perceptions which males and females hold about their abilities. There is a multitude of studies which have found females tend to give themselves lower estimates of performance than males, even when there is no actual difference

102

in real performance. In other words, even before they've had a go at a task, guys think they're going to be awesome, whereas we ladies think we're going to be average, or even below.

Now here's the real kicker! This under-estimating of ability is even more pronounced when the task is perceived as masculine! Oh crap, I hear you say! What if the entire industry where I work in is masculine? What does that mean for my confidence and competitiveness ...?

Whilst I can't cite any research which has investigated the masculine industries specifically, I encourage you to think how this may, in fact, apply to yourself. Have you watched on silently whilst the men tussle it out in a meeting, trying to put across and win their points, whilst your thoughts circle silently in your head? Have you ever looked at a job vacancy and decided not to apply because you only had 3 of the 5 criteria they were looking for? Have you ever downplayed your achievements so as not to sound "arrogant" or "up yourself"?

Well ladies, if you have, I'd encourage you to think again. Start questioning your own thoughts because guess what ... those thoughts are not your own. They are only the construct of biology and decades of social conditioning – which is totally nothing right! We need to start re-evaluating our thoughts, taking control of them and making the decision to do what we really want to do!

And if that's giving the boys a run for their money in the next competitive opportunity, then go for it! But if it's not, that's OK too. All I ask is that you always question your motives to truly understand why you do what you do.

Swearing

If you're ever in the mood to brush up on your "French", I'd encourage you to visit a construction job, a mine site or any other masculine workplace for that matter. However be warned, the "French" I'm referring to is not the Parisian kind, it's the swear word kind. In my experience, masculine workplaces seem to use a lot more swear words in their daily communications than other workplaces.

Swearing comes in its many different forms, and we all react differently to each word. For instance, someone will be comfortable hearing and using the word "fuck", but will be greatly offended by the c-word (or maybe that's just me?). Others will drop the c-bomb like there is no tomorrow and not bat an eyelid. Some people may be completely comfortable with a man swearing like a sailor, but would be shocked to hear the word "ass" come out of a woman's mouth. Wherever your internal swear-word compass sits, there is a general consensus that as the years tick by, swearing has become more common in our daily language. Even the words such as "bloody" or "God" no longer carry the same shock value as they did decades ago.

What has remained fairly consistent over the years is the greater acceptability of men swearing compared to women swearing. It has also been found that men use swear words more with their male mates, then with their female mates. Research suggests men use swearing, particularly the word "fuck" as a bonding word. However, that's not the only benefit to cussing. Swearing helps blow off steam, builds solidarity amongst workers, expresses feelings and can even reduce the feeling of pain.

There is also an interesting discussion around the use of swearing and the exertion of power from a historical sense. It is suggested that the appropriateness of swearing was previously afforded to those with power, generally speaking, white, Anglo-Saxon men. However, the exploration of this has been covered by other authors, and is not something I will delve into in this book. But it's interesting to ponder.

The use of swear words is common at all levels of a masculine organisation. In most managers' meetings, you will hear the f-bomb. Generally, if the swearer is an older man he will quickly turn to the female in the room and say "pardon me love".

For some women, this is completely acceptable and they appreciate the male apologising for his bad language. But for me, I can't tell you how frustrating this is! I would prefer he swore a hundred times in the meeting than turn to me and apologise for letting one slip. When he does this, everyone in the meeting turns to look at me (the source of why he needed to apologise), the whole flow of conversation is jarred momentarily, I feel like an intruder who is preventing the group from being themselves and I feel differentiated from the male members of the group. This simple act of apologising specifically to me when they swear makes me feel like I'm no longer being treated the same as everyone else. So whilst the man is trying to be polite, he is unintentionally doing the complete opposite. I, and many other women, actually find it quite condescending.

Whilst the older males tend to be the ones who apologise, the younger males don't seem to have the same response. The will comfortably drop the f-bomb in meeting and conversation without a sideways glance. Potentially this indicates a remnant of the "old ways"; of the stereotype that female ears are too sensitive to hear such a word and may positively fall off if an apology doesn't follow a cuss. This may also indicate the change across the ages in the use and acceptability of certain swear words. For instance, the word "fuck" has almost lost its shock value. Yes, it's still regarded as a swear word, but it's no longer reserved for the most extreme situations. For instance, if the lunch break is being shifted back an hour due to production changes it be would common to hear "you're fuckin' kidding me" from the workers. It's a mild inconvenience, but certainly not an extreme scenario.

However, there is one word that still sits on the borderline of inappropriate. It's the c-bomb. I don't even feel comfortable writing it in full. Most men are conscious of not using this word around women but will use it casually in conversations with their mates. "Come 'ere ya c*nt" or "how's it goin' c*nt" is not uncommon to hear on a masculine site when they don't think they're within earshot of a female. I've actually had a few funny moments when a man has used this word, without realising I was around and has copped a hammering of teasing from his peers. The poor bloke was late for the pre-shift briefing because someone had hidden his esky filled with his lunch. It was another classic prank being played between mates. The guy managed to find the esky and came blustering into the pre-shift room spraying complaints, insults and swear words at his mates. "You fuckin' c*nts hiding my shit, I'm gonna get you back." The rest of the crew went quiet except for a few stifled chuckles under their breath until one of the guys piped up with "Ugh … Johnno, I guess you haven't met Teagan yet". The rest of the crew, who knew I'd been sitting up the back all that time, burst out laughing whilst poor Johnno started apologising profusely for using the "C" word. The poor bloke even apologised after the pre-shift meeting and was forever courteous to me from that day forward.

So whilst watching this guy turn an interesting shade of crimson was kind of endearing, it does show that within the industry there are still some words off limits around women. However, that's not to say women don't use all of the swear words either. They certainly do. I've heard women, particularly the more masculine women, use the same swear words as the blokes. On some occasions, it's the women who swear more than the men.

Therefore, the use of swear words is tricky. Everyone will have a different tolerance radar. It's important to gauge the comfort of the group with certain swear words and to clearly set the boundaries about what words are acceptable to yourself. The first point is especially important considering society as a whole is still not as comfortable with women swearing as they are with men. If we use a swear word that an individual or a group thinks is inappropriate for a woman, it is going to hinder our reputation in their eyes. They will think less of us for being "uncouth" and "unprofessional". On the second point, it is important to set the ground rules for the types of words you're comfortable with. In my situation, I am fine with the f-word, but not ok with the c-word. Therefore, when a guy uses "fuck" then apologises to me, I say, "that's ok, I'm fine with that one, just don't use the c-word". Nearly all of the crews I've worked with are respectful of this and other than the odd individuals (who I could count on one hand) I haven't had any dramas.

On researching this chapter I've discovered speculation in the research that swearing can also trigger higher aggression, accelerate heart rate and increase adrenaline. In other words, it triggers the "fight-or-flight" response. This response is frequently observed in masculine workplaces. From angry exchanges of words, to full-on punch-ups, aggression seems to be observed in the majority (but not all) of masculine workplaces.

Aggressive Behaviours

Over my career in the masculine industries, I've experienced a few moments of dealing with male aggression and intimidation. The moments which come to mind include:

- Having verbal abuse thrown at me from a crew of 50+ electricians after telling them to take down their nudie girl poster in the crib room;
- Being screamed at by a manager in front of a group of 20 people because the IT he was using stopped working;
- Having a mine manager interrogate me on my presence, within 20cm of my face, with chest puffed and hands on hips, in front of an entire crew (who later commented on the intensity of the manager's interactions);
- A colleague using physical intimidation with his body language because he wanted to "muscle in" on one of my projects.

It turns out I am not alone in these experiences. Other women have reported similar experiences of aggression and intimidation tactics whilst working in masculine workplaces. One woman's experience was particularly awful and involved a manager grabbing her physically whilst she was crouching down to tie her shoelace and pushed her head towards his crotch to simulate oral sex. At the time the woman was so shocked at what was taking place, she couldn't even fathom an immediate response. Sadly this incident (which is actually an aggressive assault), and other experiences of aggression in her workplace led her to resign. She did not feel her complaints or concerns about the conduct of her male colleagues would be dealt with sufficiently by her employer and as such, she left the company as soon as she could.

This man who had assaulted her could be regarded as a hyper-masculine male: someone who displays excessive masculine behaviours (Laplonge, 2013). These types of behaviours can include aggression, bullying, intimidation, violence and verbal harassment, and are unsurprising to see in a masculine workplace. I'm sure it comes as no surprise these behaviours are off-putting not only for women but for some men as well. Workplaces run by hyper-masculine men can lead to terrible cultures, high turnover, and poor safety. Unfortunately though, when you have a hyper-masculine man working in a masculine workplace, his behaviour is often left unchecked. He gets the job done, he beats the targets, he drives production, he coerces the workers, contractors, unions, whoever, to do what he wants. His achievement of the goal is applauded, and no one is particularly interested in the method he used to achieve it.

Fortunately not all workplaces in the masculine industries have individuals who display such extreme behaviours of intimidation and aggression. The majority of experiences reported by women seem to involve yelling, swearing and some puffed up body language. On the plus side, there are also accounts of no aggression at all.

There are plenty of organisations in the masculine industries that have built cultures based on respect and professionalism. Where behaviour like the aforementioned is quickly addressed, rectified and if necessary removed. Most organisations are very aware of the importance, and legal requirement, of providing a workplace environment that is safe physically and mentally. They have done extensive work to ensure the behaviour of their leaders espouses this type of behaviour in the workplace and to ensure all employees follow suit.

Additional to the workplace culture is the protective response of individual men. A theme that emerged when women discussed their experiences of aggression at work was the presence of another male, or men, backing the woman up. Some men addressed the aggressor directly, whereas others provided emotional and moral support to the women after the event. This response from your male colleagues can be very useful – I know I've been thankful for these types of blokes in the past as it helps you to still feel valued in the team. Finding these types of colleagues (I call them allies) is useful for coping with a particularly aggressive environment. In all the aggressive workplaces I've been in, I have found my allies, male and female, to help deal with the stressful situations.

Of course, relying on the boosting support of a peer is not the only option. Where possible and where appropriate, my preference is to take matters into my own hands and use a proactive approach. Shari, who works in the construction industry, says she likes to address aggression in one of two ways. Her first option is to stand strong against the person being aggressive, using confident, powerful body language and tone of voice (which we will go into at a later chapter)

110

to make it clear she will not be intimidated. If she feels this first approach is not suitable (i.e. the person is too aggressive, completely unreasonable and irate, and she is worried about escalating the matter) Shari will call time on the conversation. She will "advise the person that the conversation is not being constructive" and will suggest they re-convene at a later time once things have cooled down.

Shari's style matches my own preference for dealing with aggressive people. In my experience, it is important to stand your ground with someone who is applying intimidation techniques. That does not mean adding fuel to the fire, but rather showing that their immature techniques are not going to work on you. In the situation I described earlier about the manager screaming at me due to IT malfunctions, my tactic was to employ both options described by Shari. While the manager was yelling at me, I tried to remain calm and helpful. I was conscious of his seniority and conscious of the audience watching on. I spoke very calmly and tried to do everything I could to fix his concerns. Once I'd resolved the issue, I left the room, but I was absolutely fuming. I was outraged! This manager was renowned for his sharp temper and seemed to get away with his behaviour because it suited the outcomes he needed in his job. However, I felt it was completely inappropriate to talk to me like that, especially in front of others. So, as I was sitting there at my desk, probably with steam coming out of my ears, I realised what I had to do. I had to call him on his behaviour.

At the time when this happened, I was 24 years of age and the manager was 40 years of age. I felt nervous knowing I was about to have this conversation with someone nearly twice my age. But I knew it had to happen. Otherwise, this individual would continue to dominate me and my team members with his intimidation tactics. So after a few hours had passed and the manager was back at his desk quietly working I approached him, "excuse me Derrick" I said. He looked up at me. I continued, "I would like to talk about what happened earlier today in the training room, can we please go somewhere private to talk about it?" What happened next was really odd... Derrick sighed and said, "I thought you might want to do that". It seemed as though Derrick had already reflected on his behaviour and realised it was inappropriate. So we went in the room and I gave my big speech which went something along the lines of... "I understand you were frustrated earlier today, and I apologise the projector failed on you, but you cannot speak to me like that. It was completely inappropriate. In the future, if something like that happens again, we need to decide on how you and I are going to communicate, because that can't happen again". In hindsight those words sounded so controlled and measured, but the unfortunate reality is that whilst I said my speech the emotion got to me, my voice cracked and the tears started to well up (those damn tears!). This immediately sent Derrick into a freak out (Oh God, woman tears!) and he abruptly turned his back to me. I quickly composed myself and we continued the conversation, as uncomfortable as it was for both of us. During this conversation, we learned things about each other that helped us understand why one another had responded in certain ways. This understanding helped me to deal with Derrick in the future and Derrick never spoke to me or my team in that way again. It was a long way from a close relationship, but we managed to continue working together amicably.

The most important thing I have learned when working with aggressive people – male or female – is to always display confidence, even if you're shaking in your boots. You need to try and stand strong in their face, then go have your breakdown in private (which is generally my story). A highly aggressive type will smell fear. They will want to dominate and intimidate you. Don't give them the chance to even see a crack in your confidence. They do not deserve to make you feel like shit, so don't let them. Believe in yourself, have confidence, and most importantly respect yourself enough to stand up to anyone who is trying to degrade you.

Sex Talk

Picture this....

You're sitting in the back of a drifty, crammed full with about 8 blokes, 8 eskies, water coolers, shovels, buckets, tape, pre-start books, and you're the only female. You know the guys are not comfortable with you being there. They barely make eye contact with you, and none of them wanted to sit next to you in the back of the drifty. The seat next to you was the last to be filled, and you get the impression the guy who did sit next to you would've been happier balancing on the back step. The car is hurtling down a long black tunnel; the only light is coming from the vehicle's headlights. This light is bouncing off the coal walls bolted up with grid mesh and sprayed with a white powder. The air is thick with diesel fumes, coal dust and that mystery white powder (you think to yourself you should find out what that is later on). You also think you should probably put your breathing mask on – the one you stuffed down your shirt and hooked into your bra strap before jumping into the vehicle – but none of the other blokes are wearing them and you don't want to appear "girly". So instead you try to breathe as little as possible and keep holding on to the roof railings as the drifty bounces violently further and further down into the earth. You have a lot of time to think on this trip. Everyone had stopped talking as soon as we entered the mine. We were all too busy watching the circle of daylight gets smaller and smaller as we drove down the ramp away from the mine entrance. You're thinking, how the hell am I ever going to explain what this is like to people. The only description you think "normal" people could possibly relate to is a house of horrors theme park ride. You know the ones, where you're strapped into a little cart and it drives along in the dark, with spooky dark places and unknown dangers lurking down passageways. As the drifty drives along you notice rags and hazard tape flapping on sections of the wall grid mesh. The reflector strips pasted everywhere glow as the light from the headlights touches them and then fade into blackness as we pass. The air is hot and stuffy in some places and freezing and windy in others. Water drips from the roof and splashes on your hard hat and overalls. You're whizzing past other roads which run perpendicular to yours and you have no idea where they're going. Actually, you don't really have a clue where your road is going: Other than the fact you're 200m under the earth's surface with 8 strange men in a very dark place, but don't dwell on that. Off to the side in one of the crossroads you see an EVAC station. Try to remember where that is. That's the station that could save your life if there is a cave in, a fire, a gas leak, or one of the other scary possibilities. That EVAC station contains oxygen tanks, which is far more desirable than the 20-30 mins of powdery chemical "oxygen" you will get from the personal breathing apparatus strapped to your waist. Which, by the way, looks suspiciously like it hasn't been replaced since the 1980s. But try not to think about that either.

Suddenly you see headlights coming from the other direction. You hope your driver also sees them because this road sure as hell ain't big enough for two vehicles. Luckily he swerves into the space of one of the perpendicular roads. You see the other drifty approach and stop opposite yours. It's the out-going crew, the ones that are finishing for the day. You can sense they're in a much better mood than the guys in your drifty. The drivers (who are also the crew Supervisors) shout "G'days" to each other and start swapping production and safety information. It's hard to see anyone else in the other drifty as the vehicle headlights are pointing the other way, but your eyes start to adjust and you can see the fuzzy outlines of a whole crew of men squished into their drifty. You're pondering this, and trying to hear the Supervisors when all of a sudden you go blind! You've just been blinded by a light. One of the men in the other drifty has spotted you in the back, has whipped on his helmet light and is directing it straight. At. You. You are well and truly in the spotlight. The same guy shouts out, "Hey Davo (referring to the bloke next to you), show us your hands mate. They better not be in places where they shouldn't be". To which all of the blokes in the other drifty break into raucous laughter and suddenly it's on. More comments, heavily laden with sexual innuendo, get thrown your way from the men in the opposite drifty. Still, you can't see because that asshole has his light shining in your eyes, so you flick your light on him and tell him the guys in your drifty are complete gentlemen. The guys in your drifty don't say anything, but you can sense them shifting uncomfortably. Especially old mate Davo next to you, who

115

you realise, has just recoiled from you even further, giving you an extra 3 inches of space in an already packed vehicle. The Supervisors quickly wrap up their conversation and we're off again, plummeting down the road. As we drive, everyone remains silent, and now you're thankful for the darkness and the noise. You feel like crap and don't want anyone to notice how red you've gone and the upset look on your face. Before that asshole had come along you were already feeling insecure. Totally out of your comfort zone, paranoid about trying to fit in, thinking about the job you were heading off to do and mildly stressed about the environment. Your anxiety levels were already running high. And then that prick appears with his helmet light and his disgusting comments, making you feel completely degraded, undermined and yes, a little bit dirty. You dwell on these thoughts for only a few minutes, before the drifty comes to an abrupt stop. No time to dwell on it sweetheart, you tell yourself, that's the life of a woman in an underground mine. Take a tablespoon of concrete and harden the fuck up! You've got a job to do.

This particular situation is one that happened to me many years ago when I was working in the underground coal mine. It was during this time when I started to truly understand the sexual nature of men.

Yes, I'd heard the old tale that men think about sex every seven seconds, but I'd never really understood exactly how this played out. After all, if a guy is thinking about sex every 7 seconds that adds up to 514 times per hour! I'm pretty sure that's not the case for most men, otherwise nothing would ever get done. But what I have come to believe, through my own observations and from asking guys directly, is that sex does feature prominently in their minds. As one

116

bloke said, "it's like it's constantly there, floating around in the background".

If this is the case, that means even when they come to work, and are engaging on a professional level, the sexy thoughts are still there – ready to be brought to the front of mind with a simple stimuli. And these stimuli could be anything.

On one occasion I was out with a crew responsible for putting together metal pipes. Each section was about 1 metre long and required the male end to be fitted into the female end. Now if that wasn't enough, the pipes also needed to be lubricated to fit into one another. Yes, I know ... it was the perfect set up really. As you can imagine, the boys thought this was hilarious and proceeded to enact some pretty animated scenes. I was fine with the jokes flowing; the boys were all enjoying themselves and I wasn't fazed (which probably says a fair bit about my humour – please don't judge me). But then they started to head towards personal territory (i.e. providing descriptions of real people) and I began to get a little uneasy. That's when I called it quits on the shenanigans; "righto boys, I think we've just hit the line", was all I needed to say. They all had one last chuckle, happy with the joke and said "Sorry Teags". No harm was done, they were cool and so was I.

It's not just men in the field who have their sexual radar's tuned and ready to go; the professional men do as well. A CBD office based engineer friend of mine was telling me about the 30m dash that would occur whenever a pretty girl walked past the office outside. Apparently men of all ages, and relationship status, would race across to the other side of the office just to check out the "hot chick". There they would stand, with their noses pressed against the glass, having a good old gawk.

In another engineering organisation, the blokes from the corporate office would knock off early on a Friday to visit the local strip club. A female engineer told me of this routine and explained how frustrating it was for her and the (one) other female engineer in the office. They were frustrated not because they had an issue with men going to strip clubs, but because they felt excluded from the activity. The women were conscious of missing out on "bonding time" and the informal shop talk that occurs between colleagues at social events. So they decided to challenge the status quo and join the men for drinks at the strip club. When I heard this I was quietly proud of their confidence and curious to hear what happened next. "Well, we didn't have too much of an issue, but it was obvious how uncomfortable the men were with us being there," she said. It was as though the presence of the female colleagues had held a mirror up to each of the men and forced them to look at themselves. I'm hoping it also got them to reflect on the mental images they held about women: the stripper as an object to admire, and their colleague as their professional equal. Needless to say, not every man was comfortable with this type of introspection and the rendezvous became covert. The men would still coincidently disappear early on a Friday, but without a word as to where they were going. A few months later one of the female engineers left the organisation because she was fed up with the culture.

Of course, not all men feel comfortable engaging in such an overtly sexual way and there are plenty who respond to women in a respectful and polite manner. In fact, I would suggest these subtle men are the majority. It's just the other type are far more vocal and obvious and tend to have more of an impact on both the women and men around them.

For many years now I've been building relationships with men in these industries who have been kind enough to let me know the "behind the scenes" stuff that goes on amongst men. When it comes to discussing the sexy stuff the conversations amongst blokes ranges from the downright disgusting and dirty, to the more subtle appreciation of someone's beauty. What is interesting though is when you have a group of men who are on the disgusting and dirty path, they will not enjoy having a "subtle" guy around. Apparently, if this occurs, they will stop inviting the "subtle" guy to the strip club, stop engaging him in the conversations about what they "did" to "that chick last night" and will avoid showing him the explicit pictures of said "chick". This can have a serious impact on the subtle man if the leaders of the group are of the more explicit kind. This man risks being isolated from the in-group which not only hurts him socially but potentially professionally if the in-group is responsible for making career decisions. Therefore, these men will often appear to go along with the explicit behaviour due to fear of being cast out of the in-group.

Yet, it is these men that will help change the culture of our industries. It is the good men, who want to create workplaces that are equal and unintimidating, who can have the most impact. If you know one of these men, I encourage you to recognise them. Go and tell them what they're doing is greatly appreciated. Whilst many of them might not think it's such a big deal, letting them know you recognise and respect them will help reinforce their behaviour to continue. And if you are one of those good men, I respect your courage to go against the crowd and challenge the norms which have persisted in our industries for too long!

Mental Illness & Substance Abuse

The following chapter will cover the topic of suicide, mental illness and substance abuse. If you are suffering and require support there is help available. If you are in Australia please call LifeLine (13 11 14), the Suicide Call Back Service (1300 659 467), or for people aged 5 – 25 years call Kids HelpLine (1800 55 1800). If you are located in a country outside of Australia, please seek help from your country's relevant support networks.

In a 2012 report presented by the Australian Bureau of Statistics, suicide was the 14th leading cause of death in Australia. Of the 2,535 suicide deaths that occurred in 2013, 75% were male. This made suicide the 10th leading cause of death for men. When you look closer at the specific ages of the men who committed suicide, approximately one quarter were aged between 20-39 years of age. In comparison to other age groups, this age is when Australian men are at greatest risk of committing suicide.

This trend of suicide peaking in males in their middle years is an Australian anomaly. In many other countries around the world, the suicide rate tends to increase with age. However, in Australia the data consistently shows males in the age group of 18-44 years to have the highest rate of suicide. It is also important to realise that this age group makes up approximately 65% of all Australian mine workers, which is greater than the 55% of male 18-44-year-olds employed across all industries.

In 2014, after the media reported nine suicides by FIFO workers in a 12 month period, the Western Australian Government began an inquiry into the mental health of FIFO workers. The report found that approximately 30% of FIFO workers were affected by mental health problems, compared to a national average of 20% of the community. The findings of this inquiry go on to discuss the insufficient support within the mining industry for the psychological health of FIFO workers and recommended a Code of Practice on FIFO work arrangements be developed. They also recommended that systems of work in mining organisations with FIFO workforce "take into account the mental health of workers, rather than attempting to profile or screen for workers who are 'tough enough' to withstand the challenges of FIFO" (Western Australia Legislative Assembly, 2015).

Other states and industries have conducted similar investigations into the rate of suicide in their particular industries. The Australian Institute for Suicide Research and Prevention released a 2006 report into Suicide in Queensland's Commercial Building and Construction Industry. This report found that in comparison to Australian rates, commercial building and construction industry employees were 39% more likely to die by suicide than other working-aged men. Particularly alarming, young employees aged 15-24 years of age, had a suicide rate 2.39 times greater than young Australians. This equated to 58.6 suicides per 100,000 young workers between the years of 1995 - 2001.

There is no doubt that suicide at any age and in any gender is a devastating event. Undoubtedly it is a broad social issue which requires continuous attention and intervention. For the masculine industries, these statistics should be particularly concerning as their workforce consists predominately of young to middle-aged men who are at the highest risk of committing suicide. We should be doing a lot more to understand, discuss and remove the stigma that surrounds mental illness within our industries.

Unfortunately, the traditional culture of masculine workplaces is one that is built on the "toughen-up-princess" ideology. This ideology creates a reluctance in men (and women) to discuss any challenges they may be going through, and an even lesser chance of putting their hand up for help. Through my work, I have seen wonderful men struggling to seek help. It's like observing an internal struggle between their true selves fighting for air and the restrictive grip of a culture that forces them to put on a brave face and shun any offers of assistance. In my life, I have never seen this strategy work in the long run. Sure, you might be able to tough-it-out for a day, a week or even a month, but in the end, the stress of struggling and neglecting your psychological health comes out. For each person, it will seep out in different ways: sickness, anxiety, addictions, depression, withdrawal from others. I've seen these symptoms occur in others, and experienced some of them myself when underlying psychological health is not being looked after.

Sometimes when we are in the midst of our challenges, it is hard to see what is causing our mental anguish. We are so close to it, we can't see the forest for the trees. It is usually not until later, once we are out of the woods, that we can turn back with greater clarity and see what was causing our suffering. With hindsight, we can also see how we handled it. We can reflect on the type of coping mechanisms we employed to try and deal with the suffering and reflect on whether they have been the most constructive (or not).

During my life, I have had my own periods of mental ill-health (eating disorder, unhealthy relationship with alcohol and anxiety). Ironically, I was one of the individuals who didn't put their hand up for help. I never did because I felt like I would be failing. That I would be letting down my family, my peers, my colleagues, my boss. I had sucked myself into my own ideology of masculine thinking. I needed to be tough, to "man-up" or as the common industry saying goes "to take a tablespoon of concrete and harden the fuck up"!

And boy did I do that. I hardened the fuck up so much that I pushed everyone away, neglected friends and nearly broke-up my long-term relationship. I had become cold, emotionally distant to others and to myself, and I was dreadfully unhappy. My health had suffered terribly, I was always sick, tired and my eczema was out of control! Now that I'm in a much better place, I look back at those times with a sense of fortune. "Why", you may ask? Well, each of the times I found myself spiraling down the rabbit hole of mental ill-- health something occurred which shocked me out of my tailspin. It could have been the occurrence of an illness which forced me to slow down and reassess priorities, or the intervention of loved ones, but each time I was been able to climb out of the hole. When I reflect on these experiences I find myself fortunate that life gave me warning signals and second chances. But not everyone is that fortunate. Whilst I acknowledge the experiences sucked at the time, and I certainly did my fair share of wallowing, I know that I'm a lot stronger (and hopefully wiser) because they occurred. I hope that each time challenges appear in life I can learn from them and be a little bit stronger for the future.

This approach has helped me in many ways and is something I hope will help others. For it seems that as a society we are not doing too well on our mental health scorecard. In 2013 the National Mental Health Report found that in the 12 months preceding 2007, 20% of the Australian population reported to have suffered from a common mental disorder. That's 3.2 million people in a 12-month period who had experienced either an anxiety disorder, mood disorder, substance use disorder or a combination of the three.

If you apply this statistic to the workplace it means (on average) 1 in 5 of your colleagues will be grappling with an issue that is negatively affecting their mental health. This thought gets even more concerning when we consider the type of work typically performed in the masculine industries. It's often dangerous, potentially risky and with serious consequences if something goes wrong.

Nowadays most organisations provide mental health support services to their employees and many offer an Employee Assistance Program (EAP). These programs are free for employees to access and are often available to the employees' direct family members as well. Data from a large mining organisation found that across the industry the EAP workforce utilisation rate sits at 4.3%. That is, 4.3% of people employed in mining use an EAP service. Compare this to the statistic of 20% of Australians who experience a common mental disorder each year, and the incidence of mine workers seeking help is quite low. So whilst the organisations provide an avenue for people to get help, very few people take it up.

The inquiries into the mental health of workers in construction and mining suggest that working long hours, alcohol and drugs, male dominance, job security, bullying, poor leadership, financial stresses, relationship issues (such as extramarital affairs, long-distance relationships, divorces), remoteness and isolation (as experienced by FIFO and DIDO workers) can have a negative impact on someone's mental health.

In the other chapters we have spoken about things such as male dominance which can relate to male group dynamics and hierarchy building. Poor leadership and leaders who create a negative culture of intimidation, aggression and fear are also legacy factors in the masculine industries. Relationship issues seem to feature prominently with FIFO or remote workers who work away from family and friends. The FIFO lifestyle has a reputation for relationship break-ups, divorces and affairs. This reputation alone causes extra pressure between couples, even when cheating isn't taking place. Finally the issue of alcohol and drug use is a strong feature in the masculine industries and is something I believe needs special comment.

It goes without question that alcohol plays a big part in the Australian culture and has done so since early colonial times (when convicts were paid in rum). In modern times, alcohol consumption still claims the lives of an estimated 3,000 people and hospitalises 65,000 people each year. The cost to the Australian community is estimated to be $15 billion per year due to alcohol-related harm. The Australian public is also concerned about the drinking culture in our country, with 84% reporting concern about the impact of alcohol on the community. However, 20.4% of the public admit to still drinking at short-term risky/high-risk levels at least once a month.

Since alcohol is so prevalent in our community it comes as no surprise that drinking is a common pastime for people working in the masculine industries. From knocking off work and heading to the wet-mess, catching up with the boys at the local pub, celebrating team events and milestones or simply having a "coldie" with the guy in the donga next to you, alcohol is ever-present.

Research conducted by the National Centre for Education and Training on Addiction (NCETA) found that workers in male-dominated industries have a higher prevalence of problematic alcohol and other drug use. For clarity, their definition of male-dominated industries was those that employed the majority of males and included:

- Agriculture, Forestry and Fishing
- Building and Construction
- Manufacturing
- Mining
- Transport, Postal and Warehousing
- Utilities

They found higher than average rates of problem drinking occurred among workers in construction, transportation, forestry, mining and manufacturing. More worryingly is the higher than average rates of alcohol abuse and dependence in construction, utilities, manufacturing and farming. When it comes to using illegal substances construction workers, particularly among the younger age groups, have been found to have "substantially higher levels of substance use" than other working Australians. The substances most used are reported to include cannabis and amphetamines (i.e. speed, ice).

When you take a step back and look at the data presented, one can't help but wonder about a possible link between higher levels of substance use and the higher than average suicide rate in construction. Particularly in the younger workers. However, the relationship between mental health problems and substance abuse is not simple. In some situations, drugs and alcohol improve mental health symptoms, whilst in others they can exacerbate the symptoms. Other times the substance use and mental illness can co-exist completely exclusively of one another. Therefore, one needs to be very careful when making claims about someone's substance use/abuse and their mental health.

Nonetheless, the reports investigating mental health and suicide in the mining and construction industries refer to drugs and alcohol being used by workers in the masculine industries to "self-medicate". And after spending time in both industries I would tend to agree with their statements. I have worked on sites rife with drug use rumours, have lived in camps where my donga door has been banged on by drunken men late at night and seen the look of fear in a young guy's eyes when his random drug test returned a positive. I've even seen the strangest drug and alcohol policy where each crew was required to nominate two people from their team to pee into the cup (i.e. take the drug test). This absolutely blew my mind, because obviously if you'd had a big weekend, you weren't going to put your hand up to take one for the team.

So whilst most companies and sites do have drug and alcohol policies, they are all enforced to varying degrees. Some companies are extremely rigid: I've been tested 3 times in 36 hours at one site. Whereas other sites are not as strict; I worked at one site for years and was never tested. Therefore, we can't leave it up to the drug and alcohol policies to address the excessive use of alcohol and drugs in the masculine industries. They are obviously not working. Instead, we need to look at the culture of the industry and question why there is a need amongst its workers to put themselves and their colleagues at risk.

Part of me thinks the use of these substances is to "self-medicate", to deal with all they are going through in life. It is a well-discussed topic the differences between men and women and their ability to manage emotional challenges. Women, we are told, call up their nearest and dearests to talk through the matter. Whereas men apparently huddle into their man cave and don't want to talk to anyone. My hunch is that the masculine industries perpetuate this stereotype for men and they feel they can't discuss their issues because it's not manly to seek help. Instead, just have another beer mate and she'll-be-right!

Interestingly enough, some women have reported that when they've entered a masculine workplace and built relationships with the blokes, they will often get some of the guys sharing their troubles. It's as though they have found a "safe place" to discuss the softer things, such as family issues, relationship stresses and any other worries not deemed appropriate for male conversation. I have also found this to be the case throughout my role as a Leadership Coach. Whilst as a young female it may be initially harder to gain acceptance from the guys, once you've built those relationships there is a wonderful sense of comfort and ease between us. It's as though the man relaxes, realises he doesn't have to play the masculine game and can just be himself.

Maybe that's all we really want – to simply be ourselves at work, at home and in life, and to be accepted for that. Maybe the masculine industries are not letting a large group of people (male and female) really be themselves and this is why alcohol and drug use is high. Maybe it's time we (as an industry) started to question the value of our culture to individual and organisation. Maybe if we really embraced diversity as more than just gender, and included a diversity of thought, behaviour and perspective, we would create better outcomes for employees and organisations. Maybe there would be less alcohol abuse, and fewer suicides.

Maybe it's time we started to take actions regarding this.

PART 4

Navigating the Industry

"Is there anyone so wise as to learn by the experience of others?"

- Voltaire

Thus far we have explored the context of the industries and the prevailing culture and stereotype of your "typical" colleague. In Section 4 we will explore some of the different strategies used by women within the masculine industries to overcome the challenges and navigate their way through the complicated game of being a woman in a masculine industry. I refer to this experience as a game, because I've often found it helpful to view myself as separate to what I'm going through: I am not defined by my experiences. As women in the masculine industries, we need to employ different strategies to navigate the potential challenges of our environment whilst remaining true to who we are fundamentally.

The advice contained within the following pages has come from my own experience and the advice and experience of over 50 women and men from across the masculine industries. To protect their anonymity I have given each person an alias but have kept their roles, industry and quotes accurate. It is hoped that through their stories and comments you can learn from their experiences, many of which have been difficult and challenging, and will be able to avoid making the same mistakes. Nonetheless, it's important to remember that their stories and experiences are their own and have been experienced within specific contexts. Keep this in mind when thinking about how to apply their experiences to your own situation. There is often no golden fix when dealing with the complexities of life, but the more information and perspectives we can collect the more informed our choices will be.

It is also important to stress that there is no one right way to be a woman in a masculine industry. If you don't agree with one of the techniques or suggestions, that is OK, and in fact, I would suggest

131

that is good. Because it means you've thought about the situation you were in and found a strategy that worked for you. This is exactly what Section 4 is about: Being aware of your environment, aware of yourself, and aware of the different strategies and techniques you can keep up your sleeve to pull out when you need to.

Finally, whilst we will be discussing a variety of behavioural techniques you can use to navigate the challenges, they in no way suggest you need to change your core self to be successful. Diversity is the key to great workplaces and great organisations, therefore we need people with all sorts of characteristics and thoughts. What this section does seek to do is give you different suggestions and strategies to become aware of and flexible in your actions. Learning how and when to adopt different behavioural tactics will enable you to be strategic in your relationships and ultimately in your career. This strategic approach to your behavioural style can help you to build relationships and influence a diverse range of people and situations. Whilst being authentic is fundamentally important for building trust with others, being flexible with your behavioural style will truly take you to the next level.

To help you identify the areas which you'd like to develop, the end of each chapter contains a worksheet for you to jot down your thoughts about what actions you'd like to stop, which techniques or strategies you'd like to start and which things you'd like to continue doing. There is a lot of information contained in these coming section, so identifying the key items will help you to prioritise those which you'd like to do first.

With all that being said, let's get into it...

Recruitment

At the time of writing this book, most large companies in the masculine industries are actively trying to recruit more women into their businesses. So much so, they've set quotas, targets and KPIs (Key Performance Indicators) around the statistic of women employed at certain levels. Some companies are focusing on increasing the number of women in leadership positions, whilst other companies are trying to expand their female complement at lower entry positions. To achieve these KPIs many recruiters and hiring managers are actively seeking women's resumes and on some occasions even prioritising female applicants over male applicants.

As you can imagine, this recruitment and selection practice is quite controversial. As is the mere fact of setting quotas. However, those in favour of this positive discrimination say it is necessary to overcome unconscious bias and break the pattern of like-hiring-like (i.e. male managers hiring male team members). Those in support of quotas believe that if we don't force the change, it's not going to happen on its own anytime soon.

The counter-argument for quotas is the concern that it goes against the idea of merit. People who are against quotas will often argue that in some instances, women are employed in positions where they may be unsuited or unskilled, just because of their gender. They argue that positions should be awarded to the best person for the job, not the best woman for the job.

The flaw in this perspective is that "best person" is highly subjective and depends largely on what someone perceives as "best". We all hold preferences in our mind and are often attracted to those who are similar to us. We form better relationships, can communicate more easily and better understand those who think and behave just like us. Therefore, it is easy to think that "best" is going to be someone just like ourselves and in an industry where the majority of managers and decision makers are male it is conceivable there would be a bias towards hiring males.

This concept of "best" is tied very closely with the idea of merit. A true meritocracy means people are selected on talent and ability, rather than class, wealth or any other social position. The idea that merit is the foundation of how we make our decisions in organisations is wildly believed. However one does not have to look far into the research to realise that true merit very, very rarely exists. We do not make decisions based on merit, our thinking is flawed and we are at the mercy of biases, prejudices and stereotypes. In the coming chapters, I will present research which shows that women are not on a level playing field to men in the workplace and dispel any notion that we do live in a meritocratic society.

So where does all of this leave women who are going for a job in a masculine industry, whether it be for the first time, or for a promotion?

This recent focus on gender diversity has made it neither harder nor easier for women, but rather, slightly more complicated. On one hand, you may have a better chance of getting a job in a masculine workplace compared to 5 years ago because companies are actively looking to increase their female statistics. But on the flip side if you do get the position do you have nagging thoughts that your gender played a part in your successful appointment? That it wasn't a meritocratic appointment and you're just there to fill a statistic?

And it's not just your own thoughts which need to be dealt with, your colleagues are potentially having their own thoughts along a similar vein: Did she get the role simply because she's a woman and is she really up to the task? Colleagues, peers and even the hiring manager may pre-judge your abilities before you've even had a chance to prove yourself. Conversely, you may find your skills now getting the chance to be recognised without the noise of unconscious bias. With quotas in place, managers are taking the time to review female resumes and paying attention to their skills and abilities without discounting them because they're not male.

I told you it was complicated.

As a side note, even if there is the slightest chance that your gender played a part in getting the role, I would still take the job. After all, being male has helped men get jobs for decades now so there is no shame in the pendulum swinging back the other way a little. Take that job, do your absolute best and show any doubters just how damn talented you are! By getting in there and doing a good job you will inadvertently start changing the perceptions held about women in the workplace. Let our sex be a benefit because heaven knows we've got enough challenges to deal with!

However, the good news is that some organisations are being creative in their approach to addressing this issue of merit and bias in the recruitment and selection process. A real-life example was relayed to me by a Human Resource professional in the construction industry. She explained that at her site the recruiters were told to remove the names of applicants from their resumes. This enabled resumes to be reviewed by hiring managers without the presence of gender bias. This practice resulted in more women successfully passing through the pre-selection phase and advancing through to face-to-face interviews. However, this is where the free pass stopped. The Human Resource professional reported that it was at this stage, when gender could not be hidden from the face-to-face interview, that the unconscious bias emerged once again. In fact, when it came to the interviews one of the hiring Superintendents who, when fronted with a female candidate said, "what the hell, she's a woman, what would she know about this role". Fortunately, the Human Resource professional gave him a good mouthful about his discriminatory comment. Unfortunately, the woman was still not hired.

So with all that considered how should women navigate this complex path of recruitment? Well, first and foremost if there's a vacant position that you want, go ahead and apply. Don't even hesitate. Even if you don't tick all of the criteria, put your application in and demonstrate your competence across the other requirements. The reason I stress this point is because of the well-publicised research into women's job application habits. One of the most popular findings in the mainstream media on women's confidence comes from an internal Hewlett-Packard investigation into why women didn't occupy the top positions of their company's management teams. The report found that women at Hewlett-Packard only applied for jobs if they met 100 percent of the job requirements, whereas men applied for the job even if they met only 60 percent of the job requirements. The findings of this report have spread far and wide and have been attributed to women having lower levels of self-confidence compared to men. However, this study is actually quite controversial and other researchers believe women's hesitancy to apply does not actually stem from a lack of confidence in their own abilities, but rather a misunderstanding of the recruitment process. Tara Mohr, an expert on women's leadership, believes women are more likely to strictly follow the guidelines of a job advertisement compared than men. So if a job advertisement says you need to have at least 5 years' experience in a similar role, and a woman only has 4 years, she won't apply. However, more men with the same tenure will submit an application. Mohr suggests we women need to become savvier with the recruitment process by understanding how relationships, creative wording on the resume and advocacy play a part in filling any gaps in skills and experience listed on a job ad.

So with all that in mind, what should women do when applying for jobs in the masculine industry? Well, the first and most obvious piece of advice is try to be as technically qualified for the role as possible. Depending on your career area you may require a degree, a trade, a certificate or even a short course to keep yourself up-skilled and relevant. Make sure you've got the technical or academic proficiency for the role before you apply. This is particularly important for women as research by McKinsey & Company (2011) has found men are often evaluated more on their potential performance, whereas women are evaluated on past performance. I'm not even going to bother going into the unfairness of this, but it does point out the importance of being able to promote your historical performance and competence through your job application. Follow Mohr's advice above by looking for different ways to boost up your resume if you don't tick all the boxes. Extrapolate (but don't lie about) your experience to demonstrate your broad skills. Identify anyone within the business who you can approach to act as an advocate.

Writing Your Resume

If you're unable to follow Mohr's advice, below are tips from recruiters in the masculine industries to give your resume the best chance of standing out against all the others.

- **Form your Content.** – For each job listed on your resume, you want to include your role title, length of time in that position, the name of the company that employed you and location where you worked. For each role, you should list your responsibilities, any leadership positions you held (either formally or informally), projects you worked on (including the role you played), any cost savings you achieved, productivity and efficiency improvements you implemented and other accomplishments you achieved whilst in the role. You should also list any awards you have received, memberships to professional associations and voluntary work you have undertaken. If you're new to your career, place your education at the start of your resume. However, if you have been in the industry for 10 or more years is recommended that education and skills (if you decide to include this section) be placed at the end of your list of past roles. You must decide whether adding a skills section is going to be beneficial for your application. I would suggest only including this section if you have other skills to include which have not been captured in your past roles and if it's going to give your resume a boost. Avoid including generic skills such as "communication", "relationship building" and "Microsoft Word", these are a waste of space and may actually detract from your resume. It's also best to only include the last 10-15 years of experience as this will be most relevant to the role you are applying for.

- **Identify and embed key words.** – Most large organisations and recruitment firms will use an electronic applicant-tracking system to identify suitably qualified candidates from the large pool of applicants. These systems work by picking out key words or phrases from resumes which relate to the job requirements. These keywords are first picked by recruiters and are usually found in the job advertisement itself. Therefore, it's important to carefully read the job advertisement, identify keywords and ensure you have included these somewhere on your resume. Of course, it's important to only include the keywords and skills that you can actually back up with real-life experience.

- **Present metrics.** – Using data and figures is an excellent way to clearly show not only what you did, but more importantly, what results you achieved. For example, "Increased drill utilisation rate to 94% by implementing new maintenance schedule of 20 drill rigs", is more powerful than "increased drill utilisation rate". You can find metrics for all sorts of data relating to the industry, including utilisation, productivity, financials, TRIFR and turn-over to name a few. Look at your resume content and identify where you can sensibly use metrics to present your past performance. Using metrics shows that you understand business drivers and that you know your "stuff". People want to hire knowledge and competence, make sure you show that you have both with clear metrics.

- **Have multiple versions.** – It is a good idea to consider having a few different resumes or an editable resume that can emphasise key themes in your career. For instance, you may currently be employed as a Production Supervisor, but your past roles have been within the Health and Safety function. Therefore the skills and experience you want to highlight from those different functions will be determined by the role you're applying for. Consider each job application, take your time to edit and change

- **Cover letter.** – The cover letter is regarded by many as the most important aspect of your job application. The cover letter is the place where you can tailor your application to the organisation and role, show your passion for working with the company you're applying and demonstrate you understand their business needs. A cover letter enables you to personalise your correspondence by addressing the letter to the hiring manager or recruiter and gives you the opportunity to showcase your strengths and fit in the role. Finally, a cover letter gives you the opportunity to explain any unclear areas in your resume, such as short tenures in jobs, long gaps between jobs, intentions to move to a different region and unconventional career paths. Ironically though, the cover letter is often not read by recruiters who have hundreds of applications to review for each position. Therefore, whilst you should definitely put effort into your cover letter, you should also include the most important pieces of information on the front cover of your resume.

- **Formatting.** – When submitting a job application to a masculine workplace, it's best to keep it simple and professional. Choose a font that is traditional and easy to read (such as Arial or Times New Roman) and ensure the size is between 10 and 12 with a good amount of white space on the page. Try to keep your resume between 2-4 pages and keep things succinct, whilst presenting the most important and hard-hitting information about your experience. I also recommend you ensure your formatting is readable by electronic searching and matching software by removing images, eliminating tables, not using templates and keeping information out of the header and footers.

Ok, so that's the obvious stuff out of the way. Let's now speak frankly about the stuff recruiters don't tell you. Firstly, most of them will only scan your resume for about 5-10 seconds due to the high volume of applicants they have to sort through for each role. That means your resume needs to have high impact, fast! On the first page, you should include your name, contact details, and most recent roles. A career profile or overview summary can be included, but keep it to a couple of sentences, succinct and relevant. If your resume looks messy or complicated, there's a good chance it'll be tossed in the bin. Recruiters are generally judgemental. They're like detectives who presume you're guilty until proven innocent. They'll presume you're incompetent and it's your job to supply them with information to persuade them otherwise. Make sure your resume accurately reflects your competence and your personal brand. It is your marketing tool and needs to be viewed in that way.

On the topic of personal branding, please be aware that recruiters will Google you. They will snoop around your LinkedIn page; try to access your Facebook and any other website where you've left a digital footprint. Therefore it is important that you don't have any inappropriate or offensive photos on your accounts, or ensure you have strict security restricting access to your information. On the other hand, your social media account can be used to display your social side. Resumes only provide the opportunity to highlight your work and career side. Websites, social media and blogs you have written, give recruiters and hiring managers a glimpse into you as a person. This can work in your favour if they like what they see.

This leads to the discussion around including an Interests and Hobbies section on your resume. This is a tricky section that can often polarise different recruiters. Some think it is a waste of space and can detract from the hard skills and experience of your past, whereas others think it is useful information that can give depth to your resume. For example, one recruiter informed me that she has a preference for athletes as she believes the mental and physical toughness required for athletic pursuits translates well into her industry of construction which is fast-paced, dynamic and at times challenging. My suggestion around Interests and Hobbies is to do your own Googling. At the bottom of many job advertisements there is a contact name. See if you can find out about the person behind the name. What are their interests and hobbies, and if you see a similarity between yours, include them in your resume. This does not mean you should lie and pretend you're interested in something when you're not, but rather use your interests and hobbies strategically.

Before we move off sprucing up your resume, there are a few no-no's to keep in mind. First up, don't list your age, religious denomination/faith, political views, sexual orientation, number of children, or your marital/relationship status. Also, don't forget that if you are sharing this stuff with other people (such as on Facebook), potential employers/recruiters may find it on there. Listing these items gives people another element to judge and make assumptions about. This also means avoid listing when you completed your education. If you completed a Bachelor degree 3 years ago, the recruiter is likely to assume you're young (which may be incorrect), and may work against you if they're looking for someone with experience.

Importantly, don't include photos on your resume (unless you have been asked to submit a photo of previous projects etc.). What I mean, is no photos of your lovely self. It's unnecessary and can leave you open to bias and judgement (you'll see what I mean a little later on). Finally, please ensure there is nothing weird on your resume. No strange hobbies or interests, no outlandish career goal statements, and no crazy email addresses. Whilst cutiepiekate@hotmail.com might have been great when you were 13, it's not going to impress a potential employer.

First Impressions

So now that your resume is looking shmick and making a good on-paper-first-impression, it's time to talk about making a good physical first impression. If you're lucky enough to get a face-to-face interview your physical presentation will be the next element to be judged. And yes, I'm not going to sugar coat it, you will be judged based on how you look.

When we meet people for the very first time we make judgements. It may be unfair, unjustified and downright incorrect, but that's the way most of us work. The brain processes behind this were discussed in the unconscious bias section of this book, so I won't repeat it. Instead, I'm going to share with you some of the research findings which explore how to make a positive first impression.

In the following pages, I will provide advice on the do's and don'ts. I am conscious that this may come across as though I am telling women to change themselves, that they are to blame for not fitting into the industry. Some people may even accuse me of "victim blaming". But please let me make myself very clear. As I've already said, this is not about telling you to change yourself; it is about being aware of the norms, judgements and perceptions that currently exist in the masculine industries.

There are still people in the industry who believe women should stay out of the masculine workplace. These same people tend to have their own ideas of masculinity and what a "good worker" looks like. Usually, this image does not include coloured nails, glamorous outfits and shiny coiffed hair (i.e. feminine stuff). Therefore, if you draw attention to your femininity (even unintentionally) this can challenge these individuals (and the overarching industry culture) by acting in a way that is opposed to the norm and you will be rejected. The door will slam shut in your face before you've even had a chance to prove how capable you are. By being savvy, understanding your industry, and making wise choices about your approach you will have a better opportunity of getting a foot in that door. You don't need to change your fundamental self, but you may need to be flexible. You should be aware and flexible of when you can swing between your feminine and masculine self. Once you're in the door and have built a positive reputation for yourself, you can start challenging those frustrating norms. But only once you're on the inside. I call this Diversity Guerrilla Warfare: creating change from the inside through small and deliberate acts that promote the value and importance of women in industry. There are many other larger industry associations that are trying to force change from the outside on the big, slow, unmoving beast of industries. Let them do that work, it's tiring, frustrating and slow to change. In the meantime, you need to pay the bills and the only way to do that is by getting a job. So let's explore the best way to do that..

- **Grooming.** – The level of your primping should be considered based on the position you are applying for. It is also important to consider your personal style and what you find comfortable. If you enjoy spending time grooming your appearance and you're going for an office based role you can get away with makeup, a well maintained hairstyle and some tasteful accessories. You can even go as crazy (note the sarcasm) as wearing colour on your nails as long as it's fresh and not chipped. However your choice of makeup should be a conscious decision. Research from a 2011 study found that women who wore make-up were judged to be more competent and slightly more likeable and trustworthy than bare faced women (Etcoff, Stock, Haley, Vickery & House). However, women who wore glamorous make-up (i.e. heavy eye and lip colour) had decreasing judgements of trustworthiness compared to those with a more natural make-up look. The recommendation from recruiters in the masculine industries is to wear make-up, but don't go over the top. Keep your colours neutral and subtle, particularly if you're a young woman. An older woman is more likely to be able to wear a darker lip colour as when the skin ages, the natural lip colour fades to become closer in shade to the surrounding skin. A bolder lip colour provides better contrast, but also apparently gives the message of being in charge.

- If you are going for a site based role, and particularly in a traditionally masculine position, I would tone down the primping. Playing up your assets to look pretty (i.e. feminine) in a job interview for a role that is traditionally occupied by a man may not work to your advantage. This means going easy on the make-up by keeping it neutral, wearing your hair styled simply, tied back into a simple bun or in a low pony tail. The idea around these tactics is to help the interviewer to see you fitting easily into the site environment which is usually populated by men. As unfair, discriminatory and downright wrong as this may seem, a hiring manager will be very conscious of bringing a woman into a mostly male environment particularly if she is attractive (i.e. feminine). Some of them will be worried that a pretty woman will cause trouble in the crews (don't laugh, I've heard this from male managers before). Therefore, the tactic of downplaying (but not abandoning) femininity and playing up your masculine side may actually help you in the job interview. Research found that women who displayed more masculine traits were rated more suitable for traditionally male jobs. However, this effect did not exist for women who applied for feminine jobs. Being regarded as attractive results in more beneficial outcomes for women when they are applying for feminine jobs (Johnson, Podratz, Dipboye and Gibbons, 2010).

- This research mirrors my own experiences, as well as the experiences of other women. A young female engineer shared her recruitment story when applying for a role on a construction site. She had worn a nice blouse, pencil skirt and closed toe heels to the interview which was held in the company's metropolitan head office. During the interview, the female recruiter shared her doubts that the engineer would be able to cope with the masculine environment on the construction site. She had made judgements based on the engineer's "girlie" appearance and very nearly didn't give her the job. Fortunately the engineer was awarded the role and she went on to be very successful.

- It is also worth noting that this particular engineer is very pretty. Yet, prettiness is a double edged sword when it comes to first impressions in the masculine industries. Unsurprisingly research has found that people of the same sex will often hold negative biases towards attractive people, particularly if they themselves have low self-esteem (Agthe, Spörrle & Maner 2011). It was concluded that attractive people are seen as a threat, particularly if they will be competing in a similar role or department. Another study also found that the success of attractive women is often attributed to luck rather than ability when judged by other women (Försterling, Friedrich; Preikschas, Sandra; Agthe & Maria, 2007). Whereas males were more likely to attribute career success of attractive females to ability.

- These findings seriously make you think about how to present yourself when going for an interview. Do you play up your feminine qualities and highlight your prettiest features, or do you down play them? My recommendation is to think about the type of role you're applying for (traditionally masculine or feminine), the context where you'll be working (site or office based) and the people conducting the interview (male or female). If you're going to work in a traditionally female job (such as HR), in a corporate office and will be interviewed by a male hiring manager, the research suggests you should attend to your grooming. However, if you're going for a traditionally male job (a site engineer or tradesperson for example) it would be best not to accentuate your femininity, keep make-up to a minimum and dress in a slightly more androgynous style.

- **Clothing.** – Whilst we're on the subject of clothing let's explore this further. If you are going for an office based, "feminine" role in a masculine workplace you can usually get away with wearing something polished. However, this will depend heavily on the culture of the organisation you are applying for. I once made the mistake of wearing a black suit and collared shirt to an interview with the HR Director of a rail company in a metropolitan area. I had chosen the outfit as I felt it was professional and smart looking. However, I realised I had made a mistake when the HR Director (with grease stains on his own shirt) overtly looked me up and down the moment I entered his office and informed me "we're not very fancy here". Needless to say, neither of us had formed a very good first impression of each other and I did not get the job.

In the previous example about the female site engineer, a skirt and blouse may not have been the best choice for her either. This outfit accentuated her femininity in a role that is usually occupied by men. She was also interviewed by a woman, which as you recall can sometimes lead to a more negative rating. However, it is very likely they were the clothes she felt most comfortable and confident in. This puts us in a double bind. Whilst we should wear an outfit we are comfortable in (to project confidence), we should also choose an outfit which is suitable for the role. And by suitable I mean what the hiring manager deems to be suitable. I suggest doing your research about what other people in that role wear as well as what the dress code is at the company.

The company you are interviewing with could be casual and your role could be trade based. Rocking up in a suit is probably not necessary, but wearing a crisp shirt and pants is a good option. It also goes without saying that anything you choose to wear should be clean, wrinkle and stain free and without holes, lint or stray threads. If you're going for a site based role, a construction recruiter suggests not wearing a skirt "it draws too much attention to your femininity" she reports. She also recommends wearing clothes which are slightly androgynous, fit well, covers your cleavage and is conservative yet still has good style. It is also recommended to keep colours, patterns and jewellery to a minimum.

- **Posture** – A good posture is an asset to anyone, irrespective of age, gender, role, etc. Standing up tall, shoulders back, head up creates the impression to anyone looking at you that you are confident and enthusiastic. However, research from Harvard has also found this type of body posture can actually influence how you feel about yourself. Researcher, Amy Cuddy found that expansive, open, space-occupying postures (which she calls "power poses") change testosterone and cortisol levels to make us feel more confident, better able to deal with stressful situations, more open to risk, and able to perform better in job interviews. Even holding your body in a power pose position for only 2 minutes can have a positive effect.

I have personally used this technique before presenting in front of large audiences to get me feeling pumped-up and confident. Before such an event it's not uncommon to find me in the ladies bathroom, hands poking up out of a stall whilst I stand with arms held high and feet planted broadly on the ground. It's kind of like a jumping jack, or snow angel at full spread position. You can give this a try next time you have to deliver a presentation or about to head into a job interview. Duck into the bathroom and make yourself as big as possible for at least 2 minutes. However, not all power posing needs to be so drastic and obvious. Once you're in public you can still create the same feel-good psychological effects by sitting/standing upright, keeping your feet broad and shoulder width apart and keeping your arms open, not folded across your body.

- **Handshake** – A handshake is often the first real action you can take for creating a positive first impression in an interview. A handshake shows you are confident, happy to be there and looking forward to meeting the interviewer. Well, that is, if it's a good handshake. There is nothing I dislike more than getting a limp, clammy hand extended towards me. It is uninspiring, makes me feel like the person doesn't really care about meeting and actually makes me quite uncomfortable. For instance, how am I supposed to shake a hand when only the ends of the fingers are extended and the rest of the hand is curved in on itself? Seriously, it is like shaking hands with a dead fish! So how do you create a good first impression with a handshake? First, make sure you always extend your hand in the interview, even if the interviewer doesn't. This forward approach actually leads others to form a more positive evaluation of you and the interactions you will subsequently have (Dolcos, Sung, Argo, Flor-Henry & Dolcos, 2012). Make sure your hand is firm, give a good grip, make eye contact and try to position your elbow at a right angle and lean in slightly. Give a couple of firm shakes of the hand, but don't pump it like crazy. Unless the other person starts to do that, then make sure you're still actively participating in the handshake rather than letting them dominate the interaction.

It is also worthwhile remembering that on average men grip tighter than women when shaking hands. Therefore, you can afford to apply a little extra pressure when shaking a man's hand as women who have firm handshakes are evaluated as positively as men are (Chaplin, Phillips, Brown, Clanton & Stein, 2000).

Interview Questions

So now you've passed the moment of first impressions, and by this I mean you're more than one minute into the interview. The next stage is question time!

Most interviews these days will be based on a behavioural interview format where the interviewer will ask you to describe your actions and behaviour in a past experience. This format is used as it is believed past behaviour is a good predictor of future behaviour. The good news about this style of interviewing is that you know the answer. The tricky part is dipping into your memory bank of previous work experiences to pull out something useful and relevant.

To prepare for these types of interview questions you should find out the types of behaviours and skills valued by the employer. You can get an indication of this from learning about the company's culture and values on their website, scouring the job ad for any clues of the types of behaviours and skills the interviewer wants, or reaching out to people who have experience with that company. Once you have identified the desired behaviours you should think about all of your past experiences where you have demonstrated the same behavioural set.

When thinking about these experiences it is important to recall the situation in detail and in order of events, think about who was involved, the actions you took and the outcome that was achieved. Ideally, you want the outcome to demonstrate how you successfully managed a situation, but if the outcome wasn't strictly positive you should carefully highlight the learnings and development that experience gave you. Also, be careful not to tell any stories that are fabricated or which paint you in a negative light. It may seem obvious, but I've interviewed people who have given both types of answers, and the outcome is not great for them.

Behavioural based interview questions will be phrased somewhat like this:

"This job requires you to manage a number of different areas. Can you tell me about a time when you had to manage competing priorities"?

"We expect strong attention to detail in all our jobs. Can you give me an example of a job you completed which required specific attention to detail"?

As you can see, the interviewer is asking you to describe a scenario and take them on a bit of a journey of what happened. It is likely they will follow up with probing questions to dig deeper into your answer. The reason for this is to get a better understanding of what makes you tick, but to also sniff out any B.S. you might be making up.

During the interview it is not uncommon to feel slightly overwhelmed. You may be feeling nervous and your brain will be buzzing as it sorts through its database trying to answer the interviewer's questions. Therefore it is highly advisable that you take your time when answering any questions. Let the interviewer finish their sentence fully, take a pause whilst you process the question and think of your response, and then proceed to answer at a steady pace. Be conscious of taking your time when you speak, don't let your nerves overtake your voice. If you didn't understand a question don't apologise, just politely ask the interviewer to please repeat the question for you.

You should also prepare for some of the stock standard questions which the interviewer may ask. For example, some of the generic questions you may get asked are:

- Tell me about yourself.
- What are you strengths and weaknesses?
- Why do you want to work here?
- Why should we hire you?

- Describe a time when you faced a difficult situation and how you overcame it.
- Where do you see yourself in 5 years?
- What do you know about our company?
- Do you have any questions for us?

By preparing for these questions you will be able to answer naturally and with well-considered responses.

Whilst in the interview there are some simple body language and behavioural tips to remember:

- Maintain eye contact with the interviewer when listening and answering questions. Try not to let your eyes wander off when you're thinking of your question responses, but also don't engage them in a staring death match (that's a bit freaky). Regular, comfortable eye contact is what's needed. If you're not sure what this is, pay attention to your eye contact the next time you talk with one of your close friends. It's likely you will be making comfortable eye contact with them and this should be replicated in your interview.
- Keep your face and body turned towards the interviewer and keep an open posture (i.e. no crossed arms).
- Avoid fidgeting. No one likes to sit across from someone who is bopping away to some silent techno beat. It's unnerving. So don't tap your feet, jiggle your legs, twiddle your fingers or play with your clothing whilst in the interview.
- Try not to change your seated position too regularly. This can give the impression that you're uncomfortable and

nervous. Find a comfortable position and minimise the swivelling around.

Personally, I think going for a job interview is a particularly stressful scenario. Before you even get there you're trying to guess what the interviewer wants to see and hear, you're researching the company, dreaming about what it would be like to get the role and then worrying whether this really is the right role for you. Once you get into the interview room things don't get any better. You're trying to think of the best answers, positioning yourself with positive body language, attempting to form a good relationship with the interviewer, you're wondering whether they like you and second guessing most of the stuff that comes out of your mouth! No wonder it's stressful, there are a million things going on in your brain at once. However just know that all of this is normal. I remember feeling absolutely exhausted, demoralised and depressed after a number of my interviews and it's easy to begin doubting yourself. After all, an interview is basically a sales pitch for yourself, and if no one buys after a number of interviews, it can really begin to chip away at your self-confidence. Therefore, at the end of each interview, I recommend performing a little exercise to reinforce your esteem.

After each interview, take a moment to reflect on what just occurred. Take stock of everything that happened from the moment you woke up, got ready and travelled to the interview. Were you comfortable in what you chose to wear? Were high heels a good choice? Should you have taken the bus rather than park your car with the meter running? Will you have breakfast next time, to avoid mid-interview tummy rumbles? Review the choices you made pre-interview and make note of whether you would do anything differently next time.

Now, reflect on what happened in the interview. Identify what went well and congratulate yourself for that. Also, make note of what didn't go so well. Rather than getting down in the dumps about the not so good stuff, turn this around and make proactive notes about what you'll do for next time. This list of actions and behaviours will serve as your preparation sheet for your next interview (if you need it).

Finally, the most important thing to remember when going through the interview process is that you can't win them all. Just because you weren't successful in one interview doesn't mean you're bad at your job altogether. Simply take stock, reflect, re-adjust your style and give it another go. The right job will come along. Be patient and persevere.

Recruitment Actions
(Writing Your Resume, First Impressions, Interview Questions)

Start...

Stop...

Continue...

Confidence

"No one can make you feel inferior without your consent" – Eleanor Roosevelt

Building confidence. It's a big topic in the area of women's leadership and development. Constantly women are being told to be more confident, to stop being "nice" and to "Lean In" more. It's almost enough to make you think that if we can master these things we will finally achieve equality.

In 2015, the Rio Tinto CEO Sam Walsh, publically shared his mission to get more women into the senior management ranks of his business. At the time Rio Tinto employed a workforce of 18% women with very few in senior management positions. His public commitment to increasing the numbers was wildly applauded. That is, until he followed up by saying the key to getting more women into the senior ranks was for women to increase their confidence.

Walsh received mixed reviews in the media about this comment. On one hand, people were rapt that such a global, male-dominated organisation was publically stating they wanted more women. Yet, on the other hand, his comments were interpreted by some as good ol' fashioned victim blaming; "it's the woman's fault she's not in the senior management, she's just not confident enough."

My interpretation and opinion on Walsh's statement sits somewhere in the middle. I think Walsh's comments which link confidence to senior management does ring fairly true. Yet, I hope his diversity and inclusion strategy does not simply stop at teaching women to feel more confident.

If organisations are serious about increasing the number of women in their business I would expect them to be undertaking a whole suite of diversity and inclusion actions, such as analysing their existing culture for bias, prejudice and themes, reviewing workplace policies and procedures to eliminate gender bias, committing to flexible work practices that are socially accepted by men as well as women, conducting a pay gap review and taking appropriate actions to eliminate inequality. I would also like to see them partnering with Universities, Schools and Associations to help feed the pipeline of young women into the masculine industries. It will take more than confidence training for women to achieve senior management roles in a masculine organisation.

Yet, the issue of confidence is still a pervasive theme. Just do a quick Google search and the top combination of "how to be more…" ranks "confident" as the top search item. The interesting question is why does the issue of confidence often come up when talking about women? Do we actually have a confidence issue, or is this just another excuse used to explain why women aren't making it to the top jobs?

When talking about self-confidence, it's important not to confuse the concept with self-esteem. These terms, whilst seemingly similar, are actually quite different. Self-esteem refers to how you feel about yourself overall. How much positive-regard or self-love you have for yourself. Generally, it is a consistent feeling across all aspects of yourself. On the other hand, self-confidence relates to your perception of your abilities and as such can vary across situations and tasks. For instance, you may feel confident when chatting with your colleagues but may feel particularly unconfident when presenting to large groups. It is also possible to have strong self-esteem but to still feel unconfident about a particular situation. That is, you may feel good about yourself generally, but lack confidence in your ability to solve a cryptic crossword.

It's important to clarify that whilst no significant differences in self-esteem have been found between the genders many studies have reported a difference in self-confidence levels between the genders.

For example, one study (Sainz & Eccles, 2012) found female test takers underrated their performance whilst men overrated their performance, particularly on maths related tasks. Interestingly enough, in this particular study, no actual performance difference was found between males and females. Whilst it has also been found that humans characteristically overrate their performance on past tasks, men tend to overrate their performance by 30%, whereas women overrate their performance by only 15%.

These types of findings do not surprise me and I believe has a lot to do with how society portrays women. Constantly women are being told that we're not good enough, not pretty enough, youthful enough, skinny enough, stylish enough, achieving enough and, ironically not relaxing enough. It's no wonder that we women simply don't feel like we're ever enough. Unfortunately, as a side note, it is also worth mentioning the concerning trend that is seeing men beginning to feel bad about themselves. With the rise in fitness modelling, male eating disorders and the proliferation of the pornography industry all promoting unbalanced, idealised versions of what it means to be a "man", we should be worried about the social and media messages being directed at men and women and how this is affecting their self-esteem and self-confidence.

So whilst the research has found a gender difference in levels of confidence, do women in the masculine industries differ in their confidence levels? From the respondents to the online BCW survey 47% of women reported feeling completely confident in their abilities:

- "Very (confident.) I know how to do my job and if I come across something I am unsure of I have no qualms with asking for help." – Operator, Underground Coal.

- "Very, I'm responsible for a big project and have a say on many things. The team dynamics can be challenging; I believe this is the transition from boom time when everything goes, to bust times when everything is scrutinised." – Project Manager, Mining.

- "I feel very confident in my abilities. But I also appreciate advice and positive criticism." – Truck Driver, Transportation.

- "I have felt a lot more confident in my abilities in the past 3 years. I feel very comfortable in my current role – I have strong technical knowledge and strong relationship building skills." – Human Resources, Construction.

- "I am very confident!! I have proven myself already and everyone makes mistakes so if I do no big deal you fix them" – Tradesperson, Construction.

Another 43% of women rated their confidence levels as fluctuating around the middle:

- "Fairly – though it can be challenging at times within a male dominated industry, I feel supported by the males in the workplace" – Human Resources, Construction.
- "It varies with my mood. In general it is a pretty supportive environment in the office. Speaking up is encouraged. In the field it can be difficult to instruct subcontractors as they have been in their jobs a long time, but they are generally polite and tolerant." – Field Engineer, Mining.
- "Pretty confident – been in industry for a long time so no it can be up and down." – Geologist, Mining.
- "If I am working on something I am familiar with I am reasonably confident." – Diesel Mechanic, Heavy Automatic.

The remaining 10% of women who responded to the survey reported very low levels of confidence.

- "Most of the time not at all, I feel I am under greater scrutiny than my male peers." – Electrical Engineer, Mining.
- "Not very, being a second year apprentice in a male dominated area is daunting. Not know as much as the guys can make me feel overwhelmed but overall the guys are pretty good and understand where I'm coming from." – Electrician, Mining.
- "Less confident than I did when I first started working, I used to be full of drive and ambition, however having experienced numerous knock backs (some based on gender) I lost a lot of confidence and frankly hope of advancing, I have come to accept that although I have a good job, I will probably not advance very far. To do that

163

in this industry you really need to be an engineer, which I am not." – Health and Safety, Oil and Gas.

- "When I returned from parental leave I didn't know what they were talking about in meetings. I had been out of the business for a year. I really doubted myself." – IR Manager, Construction.

The responses from the survey highlight that whilst a large proportion of women feel confident in their role, most women go through moments of feeling OK with themselves to times of complete self-doubt. This result reflects my personal experience in the mining, engineering and construction industries. Over the years I've worked with hundreds of leaders, the majority of which are men. From this pool, I would estimate 10-20% of the men I've coached have needed support and development in their self-esteem and/or confidence. Of the handful of women leaders I've worked with the majority (I would estimate 75-90%) have been battling thoughts of self-doubt and insecurity. As a side note, most of these women were good performers so had no performance-related reasons to doubt themselves.

So what can you do if you find yourself on the less confident end of the spectrum and you wish to improve your confidence? The answer to this all depends on whether you want a quick fix or a more sustained long-lasting adjustment to your confidence.

Firstly, let's look at the quick fix. Otherwise known as "fake it till you make it". Personally, I'm a big fan of this approach and have been a big "faker" on many occasions. Like the time I was asked to MC a ceremony that was 500% bigger than any audience I'd ever presented in front of before. Talk about feeling nervous! But I was determined not to let my nerves show. I didn't want to let down the event organisers, the audience and most importantly myself. So I completely "faked" the confidence and assuredness until I began to get comfortable up on stage. At the end of the event, I deemed this "fakery" to be a success when audience members came up to congratulate me on the great event and told me it was the best panel event they'd ever been to.

However, perhaps you need to fake confidence daily, rather than for a standalone event. Take for example the experiences of Heather, an electrician on a remote construction site. If you were to meet her, you would undoubtedly be impressed. She is a woman who appears confident and driven to achieve. Heather is highly skilled and passionate about her job yet she too speaks of the daily challenges that test her confidence, "of course I feel like I have to prove myself … I totally shouldn't … but I definitely do. Everyone always watches your every moment. I've had riggers ask me if I know what I'm doing. And every time you start with a new crew … it's the same thing over and over. It's so exhausting, mentally and physically."

So what are the tricks for navigating these moments, whether daily or sporadically, that threaten your confidence? In the following section, I will explore the most popular techniques for building and faking confidence.

Visualisation

Visualisation, also known as mental practice is "the symbolic, covert, mental rehearsal of a task in the absence of actual, overt, physical rehearsal" (Driskell, Copper & Moran, 1994). It is the process of creating a mental image of a future event. It involves thinking about the scene you will be in, the sounds you may hear, the smells you may encounter and the feelings that may arise. You then imagine yourself performing in the way you wish to perform. Not surprisingly, this technique is widely used by professional athletes to complement their physical training. A number of studies have found that mental "training" through visualisation can improve the actual performance of a range of individuals, from golfers, basketballers, footballers, trampoliners and runners (Isaac, 1992; Driskell, Copper & Moran, 1994). Visualisation is found to be even more effective when the task involves cognitive elements (i.e. how you would think, act or respond to a certain scenario). This means visualisation may be especially useful for performance in a work context, particularly when the challenges may be more cognitive (i.e. relationships, group dynamics, etc.) than physical.

Mental imagery is more than just thinking good thoughts and hoping it will all turn out for the best. Rather, the deliberate act of imagining a detailed scenario primes your brain and strengthens the neural pathways you want to use in that situation. By rehearsing a scenario over and over again, your brain begins to get comfortable with that scenario through familiarity. Therefore, if you use mental imagery to prepare for a scenario that you're nervous about you may actually reduce the fear and anxiety experienced in reality. In other words, it's like your brain goes "oh, we've coped with this before. No worries, we can handle it".

Mental imagery is also thought to work by activating and strengthening the neural pathways required to handle a certain scenario. When we imagine a scenario, we can usually control the outcome (unless they are recurring images from a traumatic event). By controlling your thoughts and ensuring you perform successfully in your imagination you begin to train your brain to respond in a way which leads to success.

So how can you use visualisation to improve your confidence? Let's explore the example I discussed earlier where I was the Master of Ceremony for a large event. Approximately one week out from the date of the presentation I began to use visualisation. Every night before bed I would find a quiet spot by myself, close my eyes and imagine a large venue filled with people. I imagined the noise of the crowd and how they would quieten down and look at me. I imagined the body language I would use, the energy I would convey and some of the words I would say. I imagined myself being articulate, remembering my speech seamlessly and seeing the audience engaged. I thought about a few scenarios of something going wrong and how I would respond successfully to each. My image went all the way to the end of the event when I would leave the stage and mingle with the crowd.

By imagining what I was going to experience before getting to the actual event I was able to calm my nerves more quickly. On the morning of the event, when I was getting anxious and nervous, I could draw back on my visualisations of being calm, cool and confident. Looking back, this helped me immensely.

To practice effective mental imagery the following steps are recommended:

1. Find a quiet location where you won't be interrupted.
2. Close your eyes and focus on your breath. Try to keep your breathing slow and rhythmic.

3. Try to relax by clearing your mind of all distracting and unrelated thoughts.

4. Decide on the end goal you would like to achieve in your mental image.

5. Now, begin to imagine your specific scenario. What do you see, hear, smell and feel? Are there other people around, what are they likely to be doing? Try to be as detailed as possible to build a solid mental image of the scenario.

6. Focus on how you want to be performing within this scenario. Pay attention to how you feel, the changes that are occurring (i.e. you feel confident and powerful when presenting). If it is a sports related scenario you might imagine how your body moves and how it feels when competing.

7. Through the imagery process you may find negative thoughts creeping in. This is OK. Don't get angry at yourself. Simply acknowledge the thoughts, but don't hold on to them. Remind yourself that you are in control and can choose to leave behind those old self-defeating (and unhelpful) thoughts.

8. Repeat this visualisation across a number of days.

There is no hard and fast rule when it comes to the number of times or duration for each visualisation session. Some people may only need a few short sessions, others may appreciate more. Either way, it is important to stay aware of how each session is making you feel and if you start to get bored with the visualisation, lose motivation or concentration for achieving the end task it is recommended you mix up your approach. You want to feel empowered and energetic after each visualisation.

Self-Talk

The quote at the beginning of this chapter on Confidence is one of my favourites:

"No one can make you feel inferior without your consent".

Unfortunately, we often give our consent without even realising we're doing it. This is because sometimes we're the ones causing ourselves to feel inferior by the thoughts floating around our own head.

Negative self-talk is such a debilitating thing. It can cause you to feel down on yourself, hold you back from stepping out of your comfort zone and make you feel as though you have no control over your life. Very often, we are completely unaware we're having these negative thoughts. Unfortunately though, this does not stop them from affecting how we feel and how we may perceive the world around us.

Yet here's a little secret I've come to realise … we are not our thoughts.

Let me rephrase that.

You are not your thoughts.

This may be a strange concept to wrap your head around, so let me explain.

Let's imagine your mind is like a clear blue sky. Now, imagine your thoughts are like clouds, floating across your mind's sky. The clouds, just like your thoughts drift around without you really paying attention to them. Sometimes they're light and fluffy, other times they're dark and heavy. Irrespective of what the clouds are doing, the sky will always remain there. Sometimes the clouds are so thick and dark that they cover the sun. The change in the clouds might be sudden, causing you to look up to notice the sun has been blocked out (i.e. you become aware of what's going on in the sky). Other times the change may be gradual, and you begin to feel the cold without giving a thought to the clouds blocking the warmth (i.e. you are unaware of the sky impacting on how you feel).

Our thoughts are similar to these clouds that drift around. Sometimes we are consciously aware of what we're thinking and can critically review these thoughts, other times we are not. It is during these times of being unaware that we simply feel the effects (i.e. potentially via emotions or moods) of these unconscious thoughts. We may begin to feel depressed, despondent, angry, helpless, or conversely motivated, energised or satisfied.

For example, have you ever had days when you just felt "low", without a clear understanding of why? This feeling might lead you to be sad, more emotional, irritable or even angry at others. You might pick a fight with the people you love. You could even be aware that you're niggling for a fight, but you can't seem to pull yourself out of your mood. Then, just as mysteriously as the mood came, it disappears, and you begin to feel clearer again.

For some of us, our hormones play a big part in how we feel, and they can make it difficult to think clearly again. If you are experiencing a prolonged mood that you can't seem to shake, and you feel unable to change the way you are feeling, particularly if you feel depressed or anxious, please speak with your doctor. However, for those whose moods come and go, it's worth tuning in to your thought (i.e. your own self-talk) to see whether this could be driving how you feel.

So what is self-talk? Self-talk is the conversation you have with yourself, either aloud or in your head. It could be a positive conversation which boosts you up, or a negative one which puts you in a foul mood. These conversations, sentences and words which you're speaking to yourself are just as powerful as the words you speak to others. It's unlikely you'd tell a stranger on the street they look fat, or tell your colleague they're useless, failing at their job and will probably be fired soon. So why would you say similar things to yourself? Why do we speak to ourselves with less respect than we speak to others?

If we speak these negative words to ourselves, these words become the dark clouds across our mind, making us feel low, uninspired, defeated and self-critical. It goes without saying these moods and emotions will not make us feel confident and certainly won't help us succeed in challenging work environments. So how do we regain control over our self-talk to begin using it to our advantage?

- **Become aware of what you're saying.** – Most times self-talk happens quickly, automatically and often unconsciously. This is because self-talk (and the type of self-talk we engage in) tends to be a habit. To change any habit, we must become aware that we're doing it before we can work on changing it. Becoming aware that you're speaking negatively to yourself takes time and patience. Jenny, a Project Manager with 11 years in the Construction Industry says that whilst she is very confident with her work, she is filled with doubt when she has to advocate for herself. To overcome her nerves Jenny says she will "Acknowledge that I am feeling that way, ask myself why, and support myself that I am worthy". Jenny is aware of the thoughts that are floating around in her head which are making her feel insecure and tries to replace them with more encouraging messages.

If you would like to tune into your self-talk to find out what messages you're telling yourself, you should try to catch yourself when you're lost in thoughts. Driving alone in the car is often a good place where you can tune in to the thoughts you're having. Another technique is to keep a thought journal. This can be done with pen and paper, voice recording or any other method you feel comfortable with to record your thought dialogue. A thought journal enables you to reflect on how you felt during a particular situation and to identify the feelings and thoughts you experienced at that same time. By keeping a thought journal over an extended period of time you may begin to notice themes in your thoughts. Are you particularly worried what others might think of you? Do you doubt your abilities? Are you fearful of failure? A colleague once told me that most of us will tend to have self-talk dialogues that fall under three main themes: worthiness ("I don't deserve to be happy"), abandonment ("If I do this my friends won't like me") and powerlessness ("I can't control anything that happens to me"). You may find that your internal dialogues fall into these categories. If so, I would encourage you to think about why these exist and start to challenge your own thinking.

- **Be sceptical.** – Just because your thoughts are your own, doesn't make them accurate. When you realise you're thinking negatively about yourself you should take the time to examine the validity and truth behind those thoughts. Are they accurate, or are you being overly critical on yourself? Bec, a Field Engineer in the Oil and Gas industry, says she will "Usually talk to my work mates about it to see if the same thing has happened before and whether I am justified in feeling that way". Janika, a Project Geologist in the mining industry also uses this approach by "re-think(ing) through it in an objective view (as much as possible) and ask the opinion of people I respect". Getting a second opinion to counter against your own thoughts is a good way to check whether your thoughts are accurate or biased.

- **Identify the root of these thoughts** – you may also find it useful to understand where these thoughts are coming from? Do they stem from a bad experience in the past, or from the words of a teacher or parent? Sometimes identifying the root of where your negative thoughts may have come from can help you to determine the validity of those thoughts. Are those thoughts accurate or helpful? Or are they hindering you from stepping confidently into

173

your future and if so, should they be left behind in the past?

- **Change your thoughts.** – Once you become aware of your negative self-talk you can begin working towards changing it. Taking a breath before reacting to a situation can help you to look at it more objectively. Can you change your perspective? Rather than telling yourself you've failed, how about viewing it as an excellent learning experience that's going to make you more knowledgeable for next time. What are the positives that could be taken from the situation? This is exactly the approach Kira, a Senior HR Advisor in the Construction industry, takes when trying to overcome any self-doubts: "(I) tackle them straight on, identify where I am lacking and be conscious when I encounter an experience which can help me grow".

- **Become your own cheerleader.** – Whilst you're in the process of trying to stop your negative self-talk you should also be consciously trying to beef up your positive self-talk. This is especially useful if you're about to attempt something that makes you nervous or anxious. In fact, I'll let you in on a little secret … you know that big speech I did … well not only did I do my power poses in the ladies toilets, but I also gave myself a little mental pep talk: "C'mon Teags, you've got this! You're going to be awesome!"

Personally, I think self-talk is one of the most powerful things you can use for improving your self-confidence, particularly if you're lacking in that area. The conversations that we have with ourselves influence so much about how we observe, interpret and engage with the world. However, for those who aren't lacking in the confidence area, it's also important to check your self-talk for an overabundance of the positives. In this case, you may be verging on narcissistic tendencies, and no one enjoys a narcissist (except the narcissist themselves). Therefore it's important to find balance. Ensure you stay positive about yourself, whilst maintaining humility and an open mind to learning and development. Back yourself, admire your strengths and acknowledge (without judgement) your weaknesses. Be your own best advocate and never, ever talk shit about yourself.

Find your Allies

Businessman Jim Rohn once said, "You're the average of the five people you spend most of your time with". Personally, this quote resonates strongly with me. If you surround yourself with people who are negative and judgemental, chances are you won't be feeling that great about yourself either. Their negativity will bring you down; you'll begin to interpret the world negatively and may even wonder whether they're also saying negative things about you behind your back. This does absolutely nothing for your self-confidence!

Instead, surround yourself with people who inspire you, who you respect and who actually want to see you succeed. These people will lift you up when you're feeling down and keep you motivated to persevere when you encounter challenges.

However, finding your allies can be more than just surrounding yourself with good friends. Seeking out a mentor or a sponsor can be a great way to gain exposure to leaders within your business or industry and enhance your skills and capabilities. Mentors are people who are experienced and can provide guidance and advice regarding different situations. They will act as a sounding board for you to share your challenges and may offer suggestions on how you could overcome them. On the other hand, a sponsor will actively try to put your name forward for promotions, projects, hiring etc. This person wants to see you succeed and will often have the power and connections to assist you.

Whilst you may like to find a mentor or sponsor from within your own organisation, there are benefits in connecting with one from outside your workplace. Internal mentors and sponsors can help you get ahead within your organisation, but external mentors can provide you with an unbiased perspective, expand your network and raise your profile across the industry.

Check with your organisation to see if they offer an internal networking program. Otherwise, there are a number of industry associations which offer mentoring programs, such as the National Association of Women in Construction (NAWIC), Australian Women in Resource Alliance (AWRA), Women in Engineering (part of Engineers Australia) and Australian Institute of Packaging. Information on their mentoring programs can be found via their websites.

The above tips and tricks on building confidence can assist you greatly but it's important to realise that building true confidence can take a while. You may be battling with your own internal thoughts and may need to unlearn years and years of self-talk behaviour. It should also be remembered that your confidence levels will fluctuate based on a variety of factors (situation, hormones, previous experiences, etc.).

Surrounding yourself with good people who are knowledgeable and positive will help you to develop your competence, and hence, increase your confidence. Building confidence is both an internal and external thing. Internally we need to get our headspace right, our thoughts positive and externally we need to surround ourselves with people who will reinforce the good stuff.

Crying At Work

When I was a kid it took my mum nearly an hour to convince 3-year-old me to go down the little kid slide at the park. So, you can only imagine how difficult it was for my parents to get me on a two-wheel bike for the first time! On one particular morning, Dad was doing his best to teach me. However, I was having no bar of it. Unsurprisingly, I'd gotten myself so worked up and in a tizz that I couldn't ride the bloody thing. We were both standing there at the local tennis court, me astride my pink bike, matching 1990's stack hat, tears and snot streaming down my face. Midway through Dad's attempt at a pep talk I suddenly blurt out

"I can't!"

"Why's that Teags?"

"Because … because of these damn tears!!"

It must have been hilarious to see a 5-year-old utter this statement and it quickly became a family slogan. As I grew up, those "damn tears" would visit regularly. Anything that caused emotion, positive or negative, my eyes would begin to well. But as I grew older I learnt (or became conditioned) that tears were a sign of weakness and should be supressed where possible.

Now as an adult I have a different perspective on tears and believe they are nothing to be ashamed of. For me, I've realised that tears will come to my eyes if I'm feeling an intense emotion and that they're my way of dealing with that emotional energy. I'm now learning to be more comfortable with my "damn tears". However, I'm not going to pretend that everyone else has this perspective, especially in the masculine industries.

During my years working in the masculine industries, I can recall crying on three major occasions. Two instances occurred while working on a very difficult project that had been marred by constant controversy, industrial relations issues, production delays and community concerns. At the time I was 24-years-old, stressed from filling the gaps of an understaffed team, was dealing with challenges in my relationship and was driving long distances each night to help out a family illness. I was clearly at the end of my tether and on these occasions, my emotional cup overflowed. On the first occasion, I shed tears whilst confronting a manger about his poor behaviour. My tears made him very uncomfortable and he turned his back to me whilst we finished the conversation.

On the second occasion, the tears sprang up whilst talking to my new manager who was trying to get a grasp on what had happened on the project before he commenced. He called me into his office and asked: "how are you going". Unfortunately, that question triggered the tears and they began tumbling out. Luckily for me, this manager reacted much better than the first one and I didn't feel so embarrassed.

The third occasion was when I was coaching a man on site. He was a lovely older gentleman, but a bit of a joker. Through the coaching, we started to touch on some sensitive and deeply emotional concepts that caused him to begin shedding tears. I too felt my eyes start to prickle and tears popped out of my eyes. There we were, with tears rolling down our faces sitting in a Ute in the middle of a mine site. However, on this occasion the tears turned out to be a good thing, enabling us to connect and build trust.

Most women report crying at work to be an unpleasant experience that's been brought on by a negative event or situation. According to the women who responded to The BCW survey approximately 80% of respondents reported having shed a tear either in the workplace or because of something that occurred at work. Below is a selection of some of their experiences:

- "I was belittled by a Contractor's Manager on site – I didn't cry in front of them – I went to the toilets and cried for 10 minutes to let it out then went back to my job as if nothing happened." – Contracts Administrator, Mining Construction.
- "The cause was feeling as though I was not valued or recognised for the work I was doing through a high pressure restructure scenario. I was in the office of a friend at the time, and was conscious of not allowing anyone else to see. Afterwards, I took some steps to make

179

my concerns known to a manager in a less 'emotional' way, and got on with my work." – Human Resources, Construction.

- "Sometimes but never in front of anyone and usually back at camp. Was feeling ridiculously isolated and lonely plus I'd had a terrible day with tool failures etc." – Field Engineer, Oil and Gas.

- "Lots when I'd get yelled at /when I was pregnant. I found it very hard not to as I am a very emotional person and even when I wouldn't want to, I couldn't help it. And yes the reactions to it were not pleasant" – Electrical Tradesperson, Solar Installations.

- "A colleague came to my desk and verbally ripped to shreds a piece of work I had done, it was very public. I told him I thought his assessment was harsh, he disagreed. I lifted my coat and bag and left the building and went for a long walk. When I returned (by this point I was no longer crying) my boss approached me, said he had been told about the event and discussed with me what I wanted to do about it. I later took the guy aside in a meeting room and told him not to behave like this again. I told him I understood he was under a lot of pressure at the time but that it was completely inappropriate to take it out on me. The next day he gave me a box of chocolates!! Again, I took him aside and said I did not need chocolates I needed to be treated in a fair and respectful manner. (I was absolutely furious about the chocolates. I threw them away)" – Manager, Engineering.

- "I used to cry every morning from frustration and not being listened to. I was so grateful for the redundancy." – Manager, Mining Exploration.
- "My boss went crazy at me for not understanding a company form in the first few months of being at the company. He pulled me aside and told me to stop crying; that he shouldn't have yelled at me. However this wasn't to be the last time". – Project & Design Engineer, Mechanical Services.

So even though crying at work has happened to most women, it is still looked upon negatively. As one Tradeswoman who works in Underground coal reported, crying "would be a sign of weakness". In these masculine industries (and dare I say traditional Australian culture) men are taught to be tough and strong. Real men don't cry and you're a "sook", a "pussy", or worse yet, a "girl" if you do. This social culture is often marked as one of the reasons why men cry less than women. A clinical psychologist who studies emotional tears found that women cry 30-64 times per year whereas men cry just 6-17 times per year (Vingerhoets, 2013).

Another explanation for why women cry more than men comes down to biology. It has been identified that women have smaller tear ducts which get filled faster resulting in tears spilling out more quickly. Other studies have attributed increased crying to hormones. Higher levels of prolactin are thought to be responsible for increasing proneness to crying (Vingerhoets, Cornelius, Van Heck & Becht, 2000).

So, if the science is accurate, and women do have a tendency to cry more than men, what should women do about their tears at work?

As a broad statement I would not recommend crying at work (where possible) and particularly if you work in the masculine industries. Whilst there may be the odd occasion where crying can be beneficial (i.e. to connect emphatically with someone and express your emotion), crying at work is generally not embraced. Below we will look at strategies you can try if you feel tears coming on in an undesirable situation:

- **Don't let the emotions build up** – I'm guilty of this one. You think you can handle the stress, anxiety, disappointment (whatever you're feeling), but instead it causes you to be highly strung and emotional. I've learnt over the years it's important to recognise the early signs of emotional build up and do something to counteract this. Talk to a friend, speak to a counsellor, go for a jog, take a vacation, whatever you need to do to feel more settled in your emotions.

- **Tricks for stopping tears** – depending on how emotional you're feeling, you may be able to stop the tears from building up. Some suggestions for stopping tears include, moving your eyes around, up and down (without blinking), looking up can also help. Try pushing your tongue to the roof of your mouth, biting the inside of your cheek or pinching yourself. The idea behind this is to create a strong enough sensation (such as a little bit of safe pain) that will distract you from your emotional distress.

- **Don't confuse tears with anger** – If you're feeling angry, don't feel you can't express this emotion. I've often seen women get so angry, but then feel powerless to be able to communicate this anger constructively, which results in tears of frustration. Instead, consider what is making you angry and focus on addressing this instead of getting swept up in the emotion.

- **Use your words** – Even if the tears do start to flow, you can still recover your position if you continue to speak through it. You may like to briefly acknowledge the fact you're crying, without lingering on the fact, "As you can see I feel strongly about this topic. I would like to discuss how we can address the problems". By focusing on the issues at hand you remove the focus from yourself as an individual (who cries and "can't cope") back to the issues that are causing concern.

- **Remove yourself from the situation** – If you find the tears are coming thick and fast it's advisable that you excuse yourself from the situation. A simple statement like "Please give me a minute to consider everything and I will get back to you". By removing yourself you can let the other people who are present decide how they want to respond. Those who are uncomfortable with tears will be thankful you're going to leave so they don't have to deal with it. Others who are OK with tears may tell you to stay so you can work it out. Read the signs of the other parties to see who's uncomfortable or genuinely wants to help, and then make your decision whether you go or stay.

These are just a couple of techniques that can assist you in the moments of teary emotions at work. As a closing comment however, please remember that these techniques are intended to give you a moment of control to stop the tears from showing up in unwanted situations. What I would like to stress is the importance of not bottling up your emotions consistently. I have seen this happen too often through my coaching work, and am even guilty of doing this myself at times. It is not a good place to be. Bottled up emotions can fester inside of you, affecting your mood, your perspectives, your energy and even your physical health. If you find that you're feeling constantly flooded with emotions and regularly experience crying, please speak with someone (such as a trusted friend, counsellor, psychologist or doctor) who can help you to work out what's causing your emotions and how you might be able to gain better emotional balance.

| **Confidence Actions** |
| (Visualisation, Self-Talk, Finding Your Allies, Crying At Work) |
| **Start...** |
| |
| **Stop...** |
| |
| **Continue...** |
| |

Career Management

"Why fit in when you were born to stand out." – Dr. Seuss

Being Visible

As a woman working in a masculine workplace chances are you will be noticed.

Some ladies may find this attention enjoyable, others will shrink from it. At an industry event one evening I was speaking with a young female engineer who shared her immense dislike for going out on site visits. She felt extremely uncomfortable in the site uniform pants as she felt they accentuated her bottom, which she believed was large. In her day-to-day life she would normally wear dresses and skirts to cover the shape of her bottom, but going out to site forced her into clothing she was already uncomfortable with. She then shared with me some of the comments she had overheard whilst walking around on site, which made her even more uncomfortable. This led her to become withdrawn on site and less likely to share her opinions or ask questions. Unfortunately, this behaviour, irrespective of her technical capabilities, will end up limiting her career opportunities. Although I hope the culture in our workplaces can evolve beyond those sorts of comments, currently we're a long way off. Therefore, I hope this wonderful woman learns to recognise how incredibly capable she is, to embrace her womanly curves and to be proud of her differences. Own the spotlight girl!

And by spotlight, I don't mean you need to be the life of the party. You don't need to become an extrovert if you're not one naturally. You don't need to speak loudly and constantly just to be heard. Rather, by owning the spotlight I mean you embrace the full concept of who you are. Be authentic and be proud of that because if you don't, and if you withdraw, not only will you hurt your own possibilities you may actually be helping to perpetuate the stereotype that women don't belong in these industries. By being reserved and timid we run the risk of confirming biases held by people who think women are less capable than men. As unfair as it may sound, any woman who is currently working in a masculine industry carries the weight on her shoulders of all other women, existing and future, who want a career in these workplaces.

Does this shock you? Does it sound unfair? Well unfortunately, this is still a reality of the masculine industries. I've heard too many Superintendents say "I don't want a woman on this team, we've had one before and it didn't work out" or from a Supervisor "the last girl we had was useless". Or you may have even received the incredibly backhanded comment of "you're not like the other girls we've had here before". The behaviour or performance of previous women has tainted the perceived success/failure of any future women.

So because we stand out, because we are so rare, our behaviours are exemplified. For good or for bad, we get noticed and the perceptions formed are also allocated to other women. If our behaviours are perceived as bad it's not that Teagan (as an individual) isn't good enough, it's that women (which Teagan is one of) aren't good enough. This means it's a good idea to be aware of how visible we are as women in a workforce that is predominately populated with men.

However, when we're feeling insecure and uncomfortable it can be difficult to feel comfortable in the spotlight. If you're feeling this way, I encourage you to work on your confidence as much as possible. Because you have just as much right to be in this workplace, and to contribute, than anyone else. You have the right to voice your opinions, express your needs and share your insights.

Be present and engaged. Learn about your organisation, what drives its decisions? Who are the movers and shakers in your company? What motivates them, what do they value? Develop financial awareness and look for ways to contribute to eliminating costs. Own your mistakes, but follow them up with actions to remedy any errors. Volunteer to work on different projects with different teams. Always take the opportunity to learn new skills. Put forward your ideas and suggestions. Accept the promotion, even if you're not sure you can do it.

Unavoidably you will be noticed. So you may as well be noticed for all the right reasons. Own your visibility and take control of it. Be aware of your actions and how these may be perceived by others. Choose the path that will make you look good, because as Harry Winston once said, "people will stare, make it worth their while".

Speaking up in Meetings

It is estimated that the average worker spends approximately one-third of their working week in meetings. This makes meetings an important part of your working life, not only because of their prevalence, but because of the access they often give you to decision makers. It's therefore important to use this time to your advantage by leaving a positive lasting impression. Yet, for some of us, speaking up in meetings can be intimidating. In fact, one of the things I hate most is going to meetings and not saying a word. It's not that I don't want to speak, it's often that I don't feel confident to speak up, particularly if there are other dominant characters in the session. Unfortunately for me, I have found myself in these scenarios quite often when I accompany more senior men to meetings held with other senior men. The blokes tend to have the conversation among themselves and I end up sitting there like an accessory. It's a crappy feeling that eats away at your sense of worth and value. So I decided that this had to change. That I had to overcome my own self-limiting thoughts and try something different. Here are some tips I've picked up to overcome my insecurity.

- **Review the Agenda** – Most of the meetings you attend will have a purpose. If they don't, I would seriously challenge why you're having them in the first place! See if you can get your hands on an agenda beforehand or speak to the person who has scheduled the meeting. Find out what will be discussed and identify whether you have any comments or questions relating to the topics. Jot these down and ensure you take them into your meeting. Being prepared with questions/comments will not only help you to speak when the time is right, but will also save you if you're called upon to comment.

- **Position Yourself** – arrive a little earlier to the meeting and try to place yourself in a prominent position at the table. Often this can be directly in front of the chairperson where they can see you fully. This will enable you to give non-verbal cues that you're engaged (i.e. head nodding, etc.) or that you want to speak to raise a point. If you are finding it difficult to get your point in during the conversation, try some body language techniques for getting the attention of the chairperson (e.g. by leaning in, making direct eye contact with the chairperson and raising your pen in the air).

- **Speak Early** –You will have a better chance of being included in the rest of the meeting conversation if you involve yourself early in the piece. This is often the mistake I make, as I allow my more senior colleagues to take precedence. Unfortunately, this can lead to reinforcing their position of power and authority in the meeting and all engagement (i.e. words and body language) goes directly to them. By saying something within the first 10 minutes of the meeting you position yourself as someone who will be contributing to the conversation. If you are worried about finding a spot to add your piece, speak to the other people leading the meeting. Ask them to lead you into the conversation by referencing you in their previous comment, asking for your opinion or deferring to you for your expertise. Tell this person what you intend saying so that they don't jump back in if you're a little slow to get started on your point.

- **Ask questions** – If you don't have a lot of comments or opinions on a topic you can still position yourself as an active member of the meeting by asking questions. This is a great trick to use if you're a little uncomfortable establishing your presence in the conversation. You will still be talking, but you have removed the fear of saying something you think may be "silly" or unimportant. Put aside some time before the meeting to consider the topics to be discussed, the people in attendance and the questions you may like to ask them. When you do speak up to ask your question, it's also very important not to begin your question with an apology, for example "I'm sorry, but why did we not achieve the utilisation rate this week?". Using the word "sorry" undermines your question and is a very disempowering word to use when you haven't actually done anything wrong.

- **Listen First** – the fundamentals for any successful communication is listening. This same principle applies in the meeting situation. Whilst you may be focussed on what you want to say and when you're going to jump in, don't get so caught up in yourself that you forget to listen to what others are saying. Keep up with the conversation and ensure the points you jotted down prior to the meeting are still relevant to the flow of the conversation. The last thing you want to do is bring up a comment you thought of earlier, just to say something. You could end up making yourself look worse than if you hadn't said anything in the first place.

- **Make notes in the meeting** – Keeping notes is a good way to keep track of the conversation, and a good way to jot down any thoughts or questions that pop into your head during conversation. In some meetings it may be difficult to get a word in if the conversation is controlled by a couple of dominant characters. Yet, keeping up with the dialogue and writing down thoughts as they occur, you can still provide these points once a gap occurs in the conversation.

- **Keep it concise** – In the masculine industries getting straight to the point is a valued attribute and communicating in a meeting is no different. Make sure your comments have a clear message and do not waffle on too long. Some people, particularly those who tend towards the more feminine can sometimes be indirect with their language, preferring to use more words to talk around a topic. This can not only irritate others around them, who prefer direct communication, but can increase the risk of being misinterpreted and your point not understood.

- **Body language** – We've already covered a fair bit about body language in the previous chapter. However, it is worth another brief mention in this section. If you're nervous about speaking up in a meeting, don't let your body language mimic this internal feeling. If you sit with diminished body language, such as slouching in your chair or sitting on your hands, you will be sending a silent message to the other meeting attendees that you're feeling uncomfortable. Instead, lean forward in your chair, place your hands on the table, occupy your fair share of the table (with your note pad, pens, arms, etc.) and keep your body upright with shoulders drawn back. Adopting this body language will not only help you to feel better, but will convey a stronger presence to those around you.

- **Expect and Accept Disagreement** – Not every comment we make will be applauded. In fact, it's quite possible it will be challenged by others in the meeting. This is OK, and it's definitely not a reason to clam up again. Encourage the disagreement by saying "that's interesting, can you explain that perspective a little more". By doing this it shows you're not going to back down, yet you're open to discussion, and it buys you a little more time to consider how you're going to respond to the challenge. It can also be useful to have data to back up your comment. This reinforces the validity of your idea and demonstrates the knowledge, business acumen and due diligence behind your comment.

- **Don't defer your power** – Finally, if you feel you are being challenged in the meeting, do not readily defer to someone with more power than you, such as your boss or someone higher up the organisation. Own your comments and stand firm if you feel your idea is valid. This does not mean being pig-headed and immediately dismissing another's ideas without consideration. Rather, it means staying confident that your ideas have merit and demonstrating you will not be steamrolled by others at the slightest hint of disagreement. Showing strength and confidence is important in our industries and is respected amongst organisational leaders.

Finally, if you are a person who feels comfortable speaking up in meetings I encourage you to use your confidence to bring the more reserved members into the conversation. Just because someone is quiet doesn't mean they don't have good ideas. You know I'm all for women supporting women and the sisterhood, so helping a fellow lady out by asking her opinion and referring to her experience or expertise will help not only her, but the perception of all women across our industries.

Negotiating

When it comes to negotiating, especially our salaries, we women tend to fall way behind the men.

Linda Babcock, the author of Women Don't Ask and a professor at the Carnegie Mellon University found that 7% of women negotiated their starting salaries compared to 57% of men. Yet even when a woman does negotiate, she ends up asking for 30 percent less than the negotiating males ask for. This propensity not to negotiate could end up costing a woman with a $50,000 starting salary a whopping $634,198 across a 40-year career (Marks & Harold, 2011).

So why are women less likely to negotiate than men? Personally, I have found my hesitancy to negotiate is underpinned by a desire to be liked and a nervousness about advocating for myself. It sounds ridiculous when I say that, and I'm embarrassed to admit it, but that's honestly how I feel deep down inside. But I'm not alone in this feeling, other women share similar stories of reluctance to negotiate and are often too eager to accept the first offer presented when accepting a new job. Unfortunately, there is also a mindset that your employer will recognise and reward your hard work if you just keep performing and achieving great results. NEWS FLASH! This almost never happens and you would be a fool to wait for the odd chance when an employer might do this. Early in my career, I was the fool who took on the role of two and a half people when our team went through a major upheaval. I wanted to be a good team player, to help out when shit hit the fan, but I also expected to be supported and acknowledged for my hard work. Stupid me. I was naïve in wanting special praise and appreciation. I should have gone to my boss, explained the additional roles I was completing and the projects I had implemented and was managing. But instead, I kept my mouth shut, worked long hours, got stressed out and overwrought. I felt under-valued, overworked and eventually, I resigned. In hindsight I can't blame my employer, it was me. I allowed that to happen, to get myself in that situation, without doing anything to try and change it.

Since that experience, I have vowed never to get myself into that situation again. So next time you find yourself in a situation where you might need to negotiate, or ask for additional resources, consider the tips below.

- **Understand the job requirements** – Understanding what is required in a job is the first step when approaching a negotiation. What are the KPIs for this role? What are the expectations, key duties and responsibilities? By understanding what the other party needs from you, you can demonstrate how you can fulfil those needs with your skills, experience or knowledge. Doing so, gives you power to negotiate what you need from the arrangement.

- **Research your worth** – Once you've identified the job requirements it's time to suss out how much you're worth, either in terms of remuneration or other resources or experiences. If you want to negotiate your salary, have a chat with a recruiter in your field, check out the online salary comparison websites or speak to a trusted friend or advisor who works in the same industry (or company) to figure out the going rate for your role. It is also worth researching your organisation's most recent business performance to determine their financial position. If they've achieved record profits last year, chances are you can negotiate a little higher than if the company has experienced financial pressure. Alternatively, you may want additional experiences, exposure to another part of the business, or even different types of resources. Consider what your bargaining power is for the goal you are chasing by thinking about the next tip.

- **Consider your achievements & results** – Now that you've identified the market rate for your role and have a fair understanding of the company's financial performance you can begin getting specific. What is it that you specifically bring to the role via your past experiences, previous performance, specialist knowledge or education? What have you achieved and how can it be used to the betterment of not only yourself, but for the company as well. If you find it difficult or uncomfortable boasting about your achievements, stop being personal. Try to imagine you're describing someone else's achievements, how would you sell that person (who has exactly the same experience and knowledge as you do). Even though going for a job or asking for a pay rise can feel incredibly personal ("do they like me enough to give me what I want"), you're actually just selling a product. Your ability to achieve the organisation's goals and expectations is what they are buying, and this is completely separate to your inherent self-worth as a person. An important piece of advice given by an Organisational Development Advisor from an energy company is to identify how you demonstrate continued value for an organisation. If you're looking to negotiate a bonus, usually this is considered on the work already completed, whereas a salary increase characteristically relates to an organisations expectation of receiving more value from you.

- **Don't sell yourself short** – Remember the research which found women negotiate 30% less than men? Good, keep it in mind! When you do your research and establish the salary range you'd be happy with, double check your assumptions. It would be pretty crappy to go through the nerves of a negotiation to find out you were actually undercutting yourself all along. I'd recommend testing your salary range with both men and women in your field and industry to see if they agree with what you're aiming for.

- **Don't rush your answers** – If you're negotiating the salary of a new job, avoid committing to an amount too early. This may appear difficult or even risky: "what if they retract their offer and give it to someone else"? However, usually by the time they've offered you the role you're their preferred candidate. They like what they see. Thank them for the offer and ask to have 24-48 hours to consider what's on the table. This gives you time to consider what is important for you in the role and what you would be willing to accept in the conditions. Sometimes an employer or a recruiter will ask you early in the interview process how much you expect to earn. Try to avoid answering this question with a specific amount as it will lock you in before you have all the details about the role. Instead you could try a response such as "I'll consider any reasonable offer for the right role", or if they push you further for a specific answer be more direct with "I'm unable to provide an exact figure right at this moment as the role expectations are unclear. Can we please go through the KPIs (or key stakeholders, deliverables, team dynamics, etc.) in more detail?"

- **Consider other options** – If the organisation can't offer you the salary you're chasing, but you're still very interested in the role, consider negotiating other things to compensate for the reduced income. This could include extra leave entitlements, study assistance, flexible work, role title, interesting project work, development, exposure or anything else you believe is fair compensation. Having a few extra days a year to work on your hobbies, conduct volunteer work or even take another holiday may be just as valuable as a few extra dollars on your employment contract. Prioritise what will be important to you and keep these in mind when going through your negotiation.

- **Pick your timing** – If you're currently employed and want to negotiate a pay rise it's important to pick your timing. Waiting till after the performance reviews is potentially a bad time as often department budgets have been established and you may not have as much negotiating room. By speaking with your boss a couple of months before performance reviews you will likely be the first in your team to ask for an increase and it will give your boss time to consider the budget. It is also advisable to give your boss notice that you wish to discuss your salary, rather than spring it on them. If you're going for a new job and conducting your negotiations for a starting salary it's advisable not to make salary negotiations your first topic of conversation. Wait until you have sufficient information about the role and preferably until you have confirmation the employer wants to offer you the position. If your potential employer doesn't bring up the discussion about salary, but you feel ready and prepared to have the conversation you might like to try the "weave" approach.

Premise the conversation with "that's great news I've been offered the role. I'm excited to work with the team. However, there are a couple of questions I'd like to clarify". Then proceed into the questions. The first couple of questions should be something fairly benign and easy for the employer to answer, such as what I.T. operating system does the company use, or what time does most of the team start in the morning? Then proceed to discuss your salary expectations (or flexible work, or bonus, or whatever is most important to you). Follow this up with another simple question (are there any car parking arrangements you should know about?) and then bring up your next negotiation priority in the question afterwards. This woven approach enables you to control the conversation, but does not put too much pressure on the other party to cause them any ill feelings. After all, you want to keep this person on side to reach an outcome you're both happy with.

- **Start high** – When the time is right to start talking about salary, you should definitely have a salary range in mind. This range can emerge from your market and industry research conducted before entering the negotiations. However, rather than telling this salary range to an employer it is recommended that you provide a figure from the top of your salary range. Research has also shown that presenting a first offer as an exact sum (i.e. $87,550), rather than a round number ($87,000) is less likely to receive a counteroffer. Apparently, providing a precise number in negotiations gives the perception of being informed and indicative of true value and hence is more likely to be accepted as fair (Mason, Lee, Wiley, Ames, 2013).

- **Be confident** – It goes without saying, make sure you're feeling as confident and powerful as possible before you walk in. Give the Amy Cuddy Power Poses a go beforehand and walk in there with confidence. As a side note, there is even some research which suggests drinking a cup of coffee (for the caffeine) before your negotiation can help you stay firm on your negotiation offer. Just make sure it's not going to leave you busting for the toilet due to its diuretic properties.

- **Remind them how awesome you are** – Whether you're just about to start a new role, or have been an employee for a while, it's worth having a succinct summary of your skills and knowledge for the negotiation conversation. You may like to prepare a one pager which details all of your awesomeness, including performance metrics, special achievements and positive feedback you've received. I would also suggest identifying where you have gone above and beyond the normal expectations in your role. As a HR practitioner, I found this type of information far more compelling than someone who was just performing really well within the expectations of their role. Have this information ready and use it to justify why you deserve a salary increase. Remember, this is all about convincing your employer, not waiting for them to recognise your worth.

- **Don't fear the No** – OMG, what if I ask for something and they say "No"! In a negotiation, this kind of a response does not mean the conversation has ended. If the other party says no to one of your requests don't freak out. Ask them to explain their reason for saying no so that you can gain a better understanding of their perspective. This information can help you to tailor your next request to something that will still satisfy your needs whilst also respecting theirs. If they say no, you may also like to turn the conversation around and ask them to provide a suggestion on what would be a fair offer from their perspective. Again, giving you greater insight into their position.

- **Don't make threats** – If you find the negotiations are not going according to your plan, do not make threats that you'll leave your job or will accept a role with a different company. The other party may get peeved by your attitude and will happily allow you to walk. Then where will that leave you? Possibly unemployed and with a bad reputation in an industry that although large, is surprisingly well connected. You want to maintain pleasantries in the negotiations as very often the person you're negotiating with will be your boss and you want to do your best to form a positive relationship with this person.

- **Ask for the final offer in writing** – After it is all done and dusted, and you've reached a verbal agreement make sure the offer is presented in writing. If you do not get confirmation of the agreed terms within 24 hours of the discussion I would personally write my own email to the other party "confirming our discussion and agreed outcomes from yesterday's meeting". Ask them to reply to your email with confirmation they agree to those terms to ensure you're all on the same page.

Although I have provided the above tips for negotiating, I have thus far neglected to include a glaring piece of research into male and female negotiators. It's the double standard between male and female negotiators; no matter how good you are, not all negotiators are treated equally. Researchers from Harvard University and Carnegie Mellon University found that females were penalised for negotiating, whilst males were not. Their research found that whilst women who negotiated were regarded as just as competent as those who did not negotiate, they were viewed as undesirable work colleagues because they appeared "less nice and more demanding" (Bowels, 2007). This study also showed a very clear bias amongst male raters who consistently penalised female negotiators across the various study conditions, whilst female raters showed inconsistency with their judgement.

This research is concerning, particularly for females who work in an industry where their boss or hiring manager is very likely to be a male. What does it mean for our success in negotiations? Could we actually be doing ourselves more damage by challenging the status quo and perceptions about "proper" womanly behaviour? Unfortunately, while I don't have a cut and dried answer for you, I don't think all is lost. This research was not conducted in the real world and involved parties who did not know one another. I therefore assume, more weight would be placed on the individual's inherent biases, rather than any specific knowledge about the other party. In the real world, people still carry these biases and stereotypes, but you have the opportunity to counteract them by building solid relationships prior to negotiating. By ensuring you've built a good relationship with the person you'll be negotiating with, whether that's your boss or a recruiter, you may help to counteract this prejudice. Nonetheless, this is only my hypothesis and further research would need to be done to explore this.

Once again we see that not all is fair between the sexes. And what's good for the goose is not necessarily acceptable for the gander. Because we live in a world of inequality we must gear ourselves with as much information as possible, as many tricks up our sleeve and our eyes wide, wide open. Yet, at the same time we must never ever let the unfairness denigrate our worth. Go out there and be confident in your abilities and stand up for your true worth. By doing so, not only will you be doing yourself a favour, you'll be helping out all women by challenging stereotypes and pushing the status quo.

Networking

Urgh, who enjoys networking. Not me. Whilst I've always thought of myself as an extrovert, the idea of networking amongst complete strangers makes me seriously drag my heels. I know it's important for my business and my career, but frankly, it gives me the heebie-jeebies. I worry about fitting in, whether others will talk to me, how I will explain what I do and how that will be received. I then remember all the previous situations when I've been to networking events where I've felt out of place and had no one to talk to. Not a fun situation I'd like to repeat. Yet I still drag myself to networking events because I know not going would be more detrimental.

Networking has been found to relate to the growth rate of salary over time and to career satisfaction (Wolff & Klaus, 2009). In particular, engaging in professional activities (such as accepting speaking engagements or participating in professional organisations) and increasing internal visibility (taking on visible work assignments, participating in committees, etc.) are two types of networking most strongly correlated to career success (Forret & Dougherty, 2004). Other types of networking activities, including maintaining external contacts, socialising and participating in community activities all have positive impacts on the career, but to a lesser extent compared to professional activities and increasing internal visibility.

With this in mind, it's important to have your networking skills honed and polished to leave a lasting, positive impression. One of the best networkers I've ever seen is a young female electrician who absolutely knows how to work a room. She is confident, humorous, generous in her communication style and makes you feel important when she's chatting with you. A great little trick she uses to break the ice when she meets people is to offer up her business card to clarify her name (which can be a little tricky to spell for new people). This business card is eye-catching and has a little ruler on the edge. It's a great talking point and gets the conversation flowing very easily. I have watched her with awe, working the room at a networking event leaving memorable and lasting impressions on those she meets.

For those who don't share a similar gift, below are some top tips that anyone can follow to beef up their networking prowess.

- **What's your objective?** Why do you actually want to go to a networking event in the first place? Are you looking for a new job? Do you want to chat to a particular person? Do you want to find new clients or drum up business? Are you trying to find a suitable person to join your team? Or are you simply there to mingle and meet new people? Whatever your motive is, identifying what you want to get out of a networking event is important. Staying focused on why you're at the networking event will stop you from wasting your time and wandering aimlessly looking for people to talk to. It will also stop you from getting stuck in conversations that are going nowhere. Now this doesn't mean you should be cut throat and ruthlessly end conversations you think are wasting your time (you don't know where they might lead), but you should prioritise your time to achieve your goal. Most networking events are time bound so make sure you use your time effectively.

- **Develop an elevator pitch** – an elevator pitch is a short 10-15 second spiel on who you are and what you do. It is designed to capture the attention of the listener and entice them to want to know more. Often it is a technique used in sales, but it is just as important when networking as it can mean the difference between someone passing you over, or stopping to have a chat. There are many ways an elevator pitch can go. It can either be straight down the line as "Hi, my name is Alexis and I'm a Civil Engineer on the Bigbang project for ACME Pty Ltd" or as intriguing as "Hi, my name is Alexis and my job is to improve the traffic congestion in Sydney". The former is a completely fine, albeit safer answer, whilst the latter is almost definitely going to create some questions from your listener.

- **Prepare Questions** – Being prepared is a good way to approach networking. Try to suss out who will be attending the event and come up with relevant and engaging conversation topics to have with them. A quick Google stalk may give you some information on whether they've written any academic papers, presented at any forums or are on any committees. By mentioning you saw (and even liked) their work you will give the person a little ego boost and will give you a great platform to ask further questions. Alternatively, scan the latest media for relevant and current information that may be of interest or even affecting the people at the event. If you can't find out the exact names of the people attending the event try to find out the companies who will be going. Do a little reading on each of the companies to familiarise yourself with their core business offering and come up with some relevant questions for people who work there. By asking questions you can show yourself as knowledgeable about industry and events, positioning yourself as a person with their "finger on the pulse".

- **Don't be aggressive** – No one likes a pushy salesperson. And this is exactly what it's like when you meet an aggressive networker. You know the type. They're the one, all up in the faces of the important people in the room. They thrust their business card at you before you even know what they do and whether connecting with each other is going to be worthwhile. They are so busy telling you about themselves that they don't even ask what you do, and then when you do tell them, they have absolutely nothing to say, so return to talking about themselves. No one enjoys talking with this person. Don't be this person.

- **Ask questions** – By being the person who asks questions of others you can usually begin to build a positive relationship. Most people enjoy talking about themselves if your questions are genuine and you're demonstrating active listening. Asking questions also helps you to figure out if this person might be helpful for advancing your objectives (without being too obvious that's what you're doing) and also helps you to figure out if there's any way you can help this person with their objectives.

- **What can you give the other person?** Many of us are probably in the mind-frame that networking is a situation where you seek something that you desire. That it's a one way street where you're the person in need. You could be casing a certain person's phone number, a coffee date or even some advice. However, did you ever stop to think about reversing this perspective and instead, considering what you can offer other people? By approaching people with the mind frame of "what can I do for you", it takes some of the pressure off your own networking objectives. It also has the double effect of differentiating you from other people who may be looking to get favours from others. Additionally, the person you want to connect with the most (i.e. those who can influence your career) is usually the very same person everyone else wants to talk to. They are likely to be inundated with people wanting something from them. When approaching these highly sought people it is a useful tactic to offer something different, that is of benefit to them and increases their willingness to help you.

- **Be a Connector** – Keeping in line with the message of being a "giver", being a "connector" can also be powerful. By placing yourself as someone who can connect people who you think might mutually benefit from knowing one another you increase your perceived power. If the connection goes well, you will be responsible for this great relationship and both parties are likely to feel favourably towards you. Obviously this runs the risk of having the opposite effect if the connection you arranged turns sour. When you connect someone you are in essence offering your referral. Making sure you respect and trust both parties is important for ensuring a good fit. Also, before giving out the private contact details of anyone you should check that both parties are comfortable and agree to being connected. This is just good manners and ensures you don't put anyone under pressure from an unwanted connection.

- **Know how to end the conversation** – if you're a bit nervous about networking, but find yourself having a great conversation with the person sitting right next to you, be mindful of not getting too comfortable. Whilst it might be tempting to stay talking to this person for the entire event, this is generally not the point of a networking event. Instead, talk to this person for long enough to feel that a connection and solid rapport is being established. Once this has occurred it's a good opportunity to take each other's details, commit to seeing each other again and then excuse yourself from the conversation. If you feel comfortable with this person you can exit by sharing your objectives. You might like to say something along the lines of "it has been wonderful to talk to you; I'm so glad we met and am looking forward to our coffee date. However, if you could excuse me, I've been meaning to catch up with Sally Smith all night and would like to try and catch her before she leaves."

- **Follow up** – After you've collected a bunch of business cards it's time to decide who you want to try to establish a connection with. I recommend sending an email within the next 48 hours after meeting with someone. This shows you're excited to have met them and will increase the chances that they remember you and the positive impression you left. Sending an email reiterating your delight in meeting with them, following up on any

210

commitments you made them, or providing them with additional information relevant to the first conversation you had are all good moves to make in a follow up email.

- **Accept that not everyone will like you** – Whoa, this one can be hard! Especially when you consider yourself so damn likeable. I mean come on, you're great. Who wouldn't love you! But the truth is, not everyone you meet will want to connect with you. They might come to this conclusion because of something profound, such as value differences, or as frivolous as not liking your outfit. Either way, it doesn't really matter. Although I always try to form positive relationships with everyone I meet (the success of my job depends on it) I've come to realise that sometimes it's better to just let it go. Through my career I can recall the people who just haven't warmed to me. I thought I'd been polite and was genuinely interested in them, but for whatever reason they just didn't like me. This crushes the 15 year old girl still living inside of me, but the grown up Teagan figures it's best to move on. If the relationship with this person isn't critical, don't waste your time or energy on people who, for whatever reason, have decided not to like you. Frankly, you don't have time for that crap.

These tips will help you to develop your networking skills but the most effective way to become truly comfortable and effective at networking is practice. Approach every opportunity as a way to build your connections and meet people. Take the opportunity to attend as many networking events as possible, within your industry and externally. Jump at the opportunity to increase your visibility in your organisation by working on priority projects or volunteering to be part of an industry event. Take your career into your own hands and don't stop until you achieve your dreams.

Mentoring & Sponsorship

In the earlier chapter on building confidence I discussed the benefit of mentors and sponsors. However, I think this topic needs its own section altogether. Finding a mentor is like the career woman's equivalent of finding Prince Charming. We dream of the perfect mentor who can assist us through all of life's challenges, who "gets us", challenges us just enough, can introduce us to the powerful decision-makers and help us get the promotion we're chasing. However, just like Prince Charming, these types of mentors are rare. Finding a mentor who leaves us feeling satisfied can be tricky, but it's a relationship that can have extraordinary benefits. As described by Rita a Project Engineer, "I have one (a mentor) and it has made the biggest difference in my professional life. The benefit I get from our sessions beats any development training session I have been to".

Even though Natalie has reported her mentoring experience to be highly beneficial, not all mentoring relationships achieve results. The Harvard Business Review found that whilst more women than men have mentors, women's mentors tend to be less powerful and influential (Ibarra, Carter & Silva, 2010). This leads to women getting fewer promotions, resulting in lower pay and less influence in their industry and organisation.

212

So how can you find a mentoring relationship that is going to be beneficial? Let's explore the strategies below:

- **Figure out why you want one** - Are you looking for someone to help you navigate career challenges, do you want to gain greater self-awareness, or do you want greater exposure to decision makers? It's important to determine what you want up front so that you're clear on who you want to approach to be your mentor and to reduce the likelihood of wasting each other's time and being disappointed in the outcome of the relationship. Interestingly, men tend to report their mentors provide advice on career strategy, political awareness and how to exert their authority in public. In contrast, women report their mentors tend to assist more with their self-awareness and provide advice on how their behaviours should change as they advance on their leadership journey. Figure out what you'd like help on, and then go find someone who can support this.

- **Do you want a mentor or a sponsor** - Figuring out what outcomes you want will enable you to determine the type of relationship you're chasing. A mentor is someone who will act as a sounding board, provide advice and emotional support. A Sponsor on the other hand is usually in a position of power and will provide more specific feedback and strategies to advance your career. Sponsors will advocate for you in areas they think you will succeed. Both have their benefits, however, it's been found that sponsors are far more effective in advancing a women's career.

- **Go find your mentor/sponsor** – Research suggests that women obtain more promotions by using mentors from formal programs compared to those women who found mentors on their own (Ibarra, et. al., 2010). This makes me wonder about the type of mentors we women are choosing for ourselves. Do we only approach the people who appear friendly and people-orientated whilst steering clear of the more dominant and powerful people. Perhaps our own psychology (if it includes low confidence and not wanting to bother anyone) is holding us back from finding mentors who will be able to influence our careers in a positive way?

- **Consider what you can offer your mentor/sponsor** – Whilst t's common to think that mentoring and sponsorship is all about the individual receiving the tutelage (i.e. the mentee), it's just as important to ensure the tutor is getting something from the relationship. Mentees must demonstrate their commitment to the process, to show they are actively trying to make changes and increase their capabilities. If you have a sponsor it's equally important to show you can deliver high performance. If someone is going in to bat for you, they are also putting their own reputation on the line through their recommendation. Make them look good and they'll be more likely to advocate for you.

214

- **Asking someone to be your mentor** – The approach you take when asking someone to be your mentor will depend on how well you know the person. If you already have a relationship with the individual you'd like to engage with, you can approach them fairly directly. Explain to them what you're seeking from a mentoring/sponsorship arrangement and ask whether this is something they would be interested in assisting with. If you're unfamiliar with the person it's best to spend time getting to know them before approaching them to be your mentor/sponsor. This will help you to determine whether they are the right person to support you in your goals and will give them the opportunity to build confidence in you as their mentee.

- **Communicate clear outcomes and expectations** – Prior to commencing the relationship it's important to establish upfront what you'd like to achieve. You should also agree upon the time and frequency you can both dedicate to the relationship. Usually your mentor or sponsor will be a busy person so being clear about time commitments will be important. At various points during the relationship it's good to review the outcomes established at the beginning to determine whether you're on track, need adjusting, or whether the relationship should be disbanded due to it being ineffective. Remember, there is nothing shameful about ending a mentoring relationship because it's not achieving your desired outcomes. Not every mentor/sponsor will suit every mentee.

Ultimately, having a mentor or sponsor should be a relationship of value. That is, it should be providing value to yourself as well as value to the other person in the relationship. As your career grows and your needs change you should consider how these different needs are being addressed by the relationships you have. You may find that over the years you will have different mentors, sometimes multiple mentors at any one time. This is actually a good thing, and something I have personally prescribed too. I have found immense benefit from having mentors from all different worlds and who have different backgrounds and skills. This enables me to think diversely and challenge my ideas.

As a final thought, it is also important for you to consider yourself as a mentor or a sponsor. Irrespective of your role, or level in an organisation, you have the ability to be a mentor. You are a leader in your own right, irrespective of your job title - you can influence the people around you. Therefore, be open to the idea of being a mentor if someone asks you. Look for opportunities to volunteer your time through a formal mentoring program. This is something I have done for many years and have found it to be a personally rewarding experience. I have gained immense joy from being able to help other women overcome challenges in their careers, and often personal lives, but also learnt a lot about myself through the process. Being a mentor helps you to analyse your own life, behaviours and experiences through the support and advice you give and the questions you ask of another. Mentoring is sometimes like looking in a mirror and can help you to build greater self-awareness not only in the other person, but also in yourself.

Career Management
(Speaking Up In Meetings, Negotiating, Networking, Mentoring & Sponsorship)

Start...

Stop...

Continue...

Behaviours and Relationships

"There is a special place in hell for women who don't help other women" – Madeleine Albright

What Kind of Girl Are You?

The bitch, the nice girl or the slut. Which category do you fall into? Come one, be honest, where do you fit in?

Maybe you're the bitch? The one who speaks her mind, says things that may upset others, doesn't appear overly emotional, driven to achieve goals, speaks loudly in meetings, has a strong opinion and will passionately pursue it to get her own way. Often people find the bitch difficult to work with. They don't question her competence, but they sure don't think she's very fun to work with.

Or maybe you're the nice girl. The one who makes sure everyone is happy. Who bakes and brings in treats for everyone. Who is kind, never pushy and always puts others before herself. Who likes to support the ideas of others, but would never put hers forward in case others didn't like it. People like to have the nice girl around. She's pleasant and makes others feel good about themselves but she very rarely is asked for her opinion and certainly doesn't get to influence decisions.

Or perhaps you're the slut. The one who is friendly with everyone, but sometimes this gets mistaken for being a flirt. You get along really well with most of the men, but you find the other few women at work difficult to connect with. You've had sex with a couple of guys from work and now everyone at work thinks your business is their business. People generally get along with you but you get the nagging feeling they don't respect you.

So which one are you? Don't be shy.

By now, I hope you've realised these three characters are written with a fair bit of sarcasm! However they allude to some unfortunate truths about being a woman, not only in a masculine environment, but in the workforce in general. For whatever reason, society still finds the need to place women into a clearly identifiable and understandable box. She's either a nice girl who doesn't rock the boat, the pain in the arse who is pushy and bossy, or the one no one takes seriously but enjoys having around because she's a bit of fun.

Now I'm not going to suggest that these are the finite stereotypes women get labelled with, but they are the most prevalent. The concept of women being either good or bad, saintly or evil, stems as far back as medieval literature, and more recently to Sigmund Freud's psychology and to the discussions held in feminist literature.

Personally, I have encountered these stereotypes numerous times in my life. Early on I was labelled a "bossy" teenage girl. When I first went to college I met new friends who, after hanging out with me for a few weeks remarked with a chuckle, "geeze we thought you were a nice girl Teagan", after seeing my more competitive, dominant side.

In my experience as soon as a "nice girl" starts to show another side of herself, people don't know how to handle it. So rather than accepting it as another facet of being a girl, they have to label and demonise the behaviour. This does not occur for men. A man can be fun, friendly and engaging, but as soon as he turns serious, demanding and direct, that's OK; he's just being a guy. And that is acceptable.

Research backs up this double standard and has given it its own name: The Double Bind. The Double Bind refers to the situation where women in leadership are perceived as either competent or liked, but rarely both (Catalyst, 2007). I would take it further to suggest from my own anecdotal observations this double bind applies to women across all levels of an organisation as well as institutions and social relationships. When a woman displays behaviours that are characteristically masculine, such as assertiveness, self-promotion and direct communication, she is seen as competent, yet less likeable. In very basic terms it means that they respect you for doing your job, but no one wants to be your friend.

"OK", you might be thinking "I can handle not being liked by my colleagues as long as they respect my abilities and think I'm good at my job". Unfortunately though, it doesn't turn out this way, not for women anyway. Even if you're perceived as not very "nice", yet competent at your job, you still won't get ahead as others will distrust you because they haven't formed positive relationships and hence, won't be influenced by you. This stems from the social belief that women are all about relationships and caring about others and when a female is perceived not to fit this stereotype, she may be punished by social exclusion.

This double-bind means that women have to be nice so that others feel comfortable with them (because she is acting according to social

220

expectation). However, the kicker with this is when she is perceived as nice (and fitting into social norms) she runs the risk of being disregarded as being "too nice" and cast aside for leadership positions. This limits the woman's career progression, will limit how much she can influence her organisation and her industry and will certainly limit how much money she can make in her career.

I believe this Double Bind is part of the reason women aren't reaching senior leadership positions. When a woman's performance is assessed the double bind is very likely playing out unconsciously in the rater's mind. This means performance reviews are not conducted equally or unbiasedly as women are being held to different expectations than men. A study reported by Forbes found that across 248 performance reviews conducted on both women and men, the women's reviews had disproportionately more critical comments compared to the men's (Snyder, 2014). It was found that 87.9% of the females' reviews contained critical feedback, whilst only 58.9% of the males' reviews contained critical feedback. However, the bias doesn't stop there as the type of critical feedback received was different between the genders too. Men were given feedback about developing additional skills, whilst women received this feedback plus an additional critical element: Negative Personality Criticism (Synder, 2014).

Negative Personality Criticism is where the reviewer is making comment on *how* the women went about the task, not *what* she achieved in the task. It focuses on her behaviour, her attitude and relationships with others and whether she is being too abrasive, too judgemental, or not supportive enough. The feedback also included comments on whether she was being emotional or irrational when

221

she disagreed with something or was presenting an alternative point of view.

Now if these results aren't enough to piss you off, let me share with you the next finding. The gender of the manager made no difference to the types of feedback given to males or females. This means we women are just as guilty of rating female colleagues in a biased and unequal manner as men are.

I could give a speech about supporting the sisterhood but I'm not going to because maybe we're unaware of what we're doing. Maybe it's not intentional that we're being overly critical of women. After all, most unconscious bias is not intentional, that's why it's unconscious. But now we don't have an excuse. Now you've been informed. Now you have a choice to be more aware and less biased in your ratings of colleagues or subordinates.

This paradigm of fitting women into the bitch, good girl or slut role, is something we women should all be aware of. Yes, it's unfair, yes it sucks that we get judged in this way, but the fact of the matter is, we do. Therefore, we need to be aware of how our behaviour is being interpreted by others. Check your performance reviews or ask a trusted friend or manager for some honest feedback. Although the feedback you get from others is only their perception, you must remember that their perception is their reality. That means even if people perceive you in a certain way (but you don't think of yourself in the same way) it kind of doesn't matter. Their perception is their reality and they will engage with you in a way which supports their reality. This in turn may impact on your reality. For example, if someone thinks you're too much of a "nice girl" they may be reluctant to assign you to a project with difficult stakeholder relations. I've seen this play out in the recruitment world where women get passed over for jobs, or at the assignment of projects where men get given the more challenging and high profile tasks.

So what does all this mean? Frankly, you need to be smart. As a woman, you're juggling a lot more complexity than a man. Be mindful of this. If you care about having influence and control over your career (and frankly, across your life), it's important to have an understanding of what others think of you, and decide whether their perception is going to support the outcomes you're chasing. If the person has little influence over your career or life, then you can choose to take what you will from their opinion. Maybe they don't have much influence, and as such you decide not to let their opinion affect you. However, if this person has significant influence over your future success you have two options: one is to remove yourself from their influence (i.e. find another job, start your own business on the side, build relationships with other key people, etc.). Or, if this is not possible then you are left with option two, adapting your behaviour to create a positive image in their mind. This may involve being flexible with your communication and behavioural style and in your relationships, but it in no way means you should change your core self or compromise your values. Once again, it is simply about being savvy and developing a number of different tactics to get the outcomes you're chasing.

Sex and Relationships at Work

Frankly, I couldn't write a book about women in masculine environments without talking about sex and relationships. In Part 2 of this book, I discussed the sexual nature of men in these industries. Therefore, it's only fitting to discuss how women interact with this nature.

Sex and dating in the workplace is tricky at the best of times. However, when you're a minority female, particularly on a remote site, you will get a lot of attention. Often it may not even be explicit attention (i.e. direct flirting, pick-up lines, direct conversation etc.). It can be as simple as walking through the dry mess (i.e. the kitchen dining room) or walking past the wet mess (i.e. the bar) and having a large percentage of the men look at you as you pass by.

This attention can often be intimidating and downright creepy. It can make your skin crawl and you might want to high-tail it out of there as soon as possible. Yet this attention can sometimes be flattering and make you feel special. Or it can lead to a full-blown relationship that could lead to marriage and kids.

Therefore, the rules about relationships and sex on site are not black-and-white. There are so many variables and factors to consider depending on where you work and with whom you work. On some sites, it's going to be completely fine to strike up a relationship with a colleague, but at another, you could quickly become the centre of gossip and jokes.

A young woman who had worked for many years in an underground mine shared her at-work relationship experience with me. This woman had struck up a relationship with one of the men in a different crew to hers. Both of them were serious about each other but realised that to survive on site they needed to keep their relationship a secret. She explained that if people found out they were dating, her boyfriend would cop teasing and dirty comments from his workmates, whilst she would very likely have received unwanted attention from the other men on site. They managed to keep their relationship secret for months, but the stress of the situation, plus the additional challenge of being a woman in an underground mine, led them to change jobs. Both successfully applied for positions in an open cut mine and ended up moving away. Many years later they are still a couple, happily working on a site where everyone knows they are in a relationship.

Another woman also reported a bad experience after sleeping with a guy from work. Val, an engineer, recounted a story from early in her career, "I pretty much got liquored up and taken advantage of when I was a Vacation Student ... it was horrible. Everyone knew the next morning and the guy was a dick".

However, bad experiences don't only occur by sleeping with someone. Truck driver Kiri shared her story of a first date with someone from work; "It didn't go well. When he asked me for a second date I politely turned him down, so he took a shit on my car. Seriously! I'm not kidding. He got fired, and that was the only time I dated someone I worked with".

However, you don't necessarily need to be going on dates or having sex with anyone at site to get unwanted attention. Sometimes the attention just follows you because you're female. A young Supervisor at an open cut mine told me how one evening she caught someone trying to peep through the bathroom window to her donga (which was quite a feat considering the windows were well above head height). She told her Supervisor the next day and they immediately arranged to move her into a different room. However, since the "peeping-Tom" could not be identified no action could be taken to prevent this person from doing it again. I've even had my own encounter with a drunken guy trying to get into my donga late at night. I awoke to hear the security screen being swung open and someone yanking at the door handle. I sprang out of bed, raced over to the door and bashed back from the inside yelling "wrong room, piss off" in my very best deep, masculine-sounding voice. The guy buggered off, but it's fair to say I was pretty unsettled.

Now I'm sure these experiences are the exception rather than the norm, and there are plenty of women who haven't experienced any troubles whilst working in a masculine industry. Yet, I feel it's important to still be aware of what happens occasionally so you can be better prepared and can make informed choices. This in no way means women should or should not behave in certain ways, nor should we be "victim blaming" if a woman finds herself in an unwanted or awful situation. Rather it's about explaining the risks and discussing ways of minimising risk to yourself, whilst still working towards punishing and changing the behaviour of perpetrators. Every woman has the right to make choices for herself and to be safe. Below are points and recommendations provided by women who have reflected on their own experiences and would like to share their personal stories to assist others to navigate sex and relationships at work.

- **Watch your behaviour** - By this, they essentially mean being careful about the signals you're sending out. You may be intending to send out the friendly vibe, but could your smiles, laughter, body language or banter be misconstrued as wanting something more? Linda, a

Health and Safety professional with national and international experience in oil and gas, civil construction, military and mining experience believes finding a balance between being "flirty and friendly" is very important. "You're always in the news, so be careful what you do and say" she says. This was something I learnt early in my career after a couple of different situations where men became a little too interested and eager to build a "friendship". I had been my usual smiling, chatty self with everyone on site, but I began to get the vibe from these blokes that they were looking for more than friendship. Since I was completely disinterested I became extra careful about my behaviour around them and was very clear and intentional with my messages. However, this does not mean you can't be mates with the blokes on site. I've developed some great platonic friendships across the years. You just need to be aware of how your behaviour is being interpreted and what the motivations are of the other party. If you're on the same page that's great, but if not, perhaps you might want to clarify your position.

- **Set boundaries** - You've probably heard someone say before that guys don't pick up cues very well, so you need to tell it to them straight, no beating around the bush. If someone does or says something you're not comfortable with, tell them. If they are being inappropriate, tell them. I know being direct may not be easy at times, but telling the offending person exactly how you feel is the only way to do it. No one has the right to make you feel awful, uncomfortable or insecure, no matter their position. Right

227

from the beginning of your interactions with people it's important to set the boundaries of what you're ok with. I'm not suggesting you sit them down and give a PowerPoint presentation about "What's OK By Me", but you do need to let them know when they've crossed a line.

- **Tone down the "girliness"** - This is an interesting piece of advice given by women in various roles, from engineers, human resource professionals to tradespeople. By this they mean downplaying your overtly female characteristics. For instance, wearing minimal makeup, modest jewellery, loose clothing and tying your hair back are all strategies used by women to appear less "female", and hopefully to be viewed less sexually. The rationale is covered extensively in the New York Times, Wall Street Journal and Businessweek bestseller "Nice Girls Don't Get the Corner Office 101: Unconscious Mistakes Women Make That Sabotage Their Careers" by Lois P. Frankel. Personally, I find adopting a more androgynous look when I'm new to a site, makes me feel more comfortable amongst the men. Then, as I build trusting, professional relationships with them I begin to inject more of my feminine personality into my appearance. This tactic works for me, but it may not work for others. Pick and choose what works best for you.

- **"Don't screw the crew"** - This advice comes from a number of young women after they had slept with a person at work. The scenario for each woman was different, from consensual relationships to alcohol fuelled next-day-regrets, but the outcome was similar: rumour and reputation of being a "slut". Now not all workplace relationships end this way (and in fact there are quite a number which have been successful and long-term) but as soon as you decide to sleep with a co-worker in a masculine environment, you are playing with fire. Particularly if you don't know them very well. There is a risk that the person you slept with will tell the rest of the crew, which will then be told to other people, who will then tell others. News on a mine site, particularly one with a residential camp, spreads like wildfire, particularly if the gossip and rumour is about a woman's sexuality. As we know, men's sexual activities don't get the same scrutiny. Couple this with the fact that you're "always in the news" (to quote Linda from above) and it's the perfect storm. The resulting rumours can be devastating for a woman professionally, mentally and physically. Women have reported other men approaching them for sex, trying to break into their dongas, comments being yelled at them across site, developing anxiety from the situation and even quitting their jobs and moving towns. It is an unfair reality that women still get judged for our sexual choices. Therefore, if you do sleep with a man from work, be aware that the comments about him are potentially going to be very different than the ones made about you.

- **It's not the real world -** In a lot of masculine workplaces, it's common to work 12+ hours per day, in remote site locations away from partners and families. A bit of flirtation can spice things up and break the monotony of work. I get it, it's flattering, but much like sleeping with a guy, it can be risky. I was discussing this topic with a group of young male tradies and this was their response, "it's like, just because there's a girl on site, the guys will pay her attention. It doesn't matter what she looks like, they'll just flirt with her because she's female". They then went on to tell me that back in the real world (i.e. home) "you wouldn't even look at her twice". Charming. Working on a remote site can be quite insular. It's very easy for your whole existence for the time you're at work (which can be multiple week's straight) is wound up in work. You work 12+ hours with the same people, you ride the bus home together, you eat at the communal mess together, you go to the gym together, you sleep near one another (but in separate dongas, usually). It's like the adult version of a school camp. Scary thought! The attention you get at site, whilst titillating, may not be genuine. Take your time, assess the situation in its entirety and then make your move with awareness.

- **Recognise the Stereotypes & Perceptions** - As a final note, I want to share with you another stereotype about women in the masculine industries. Occasionally I've come across comments from men who talk about women as "serial husband hunters". The women they are referring to are often workers on a mine or construction site who have been married multiple times to men within the industry. The perception around these women is that they only joined the industry to find themselves a rich husband,

230

lock him down with a kid and then divorce him. Similarly, there is also a cultural perception of having a "site wife" or "site husband". This is where a fly-in, fly-out worker has an affair with someone else on site, but returns to their partner/family on their days off. I have not personally come across anyone engaging in this type of behaviour, but there is definitely the perception that this occur on site. And you know what they say… where there is smoke, there is usually fire. By being aware of these stereotypes you can make an informed choice about how you want to handle your own situations.

So far, we've talked a lot about unwanted advances but we also need to talk about those encounters which have resulted in relationships. Of the women who responded to The BCW survey, two thirds have entered a relationship with someone at work. Of this group, nearly 40% ended up getting married. Therefore not all romantic or sexual encounters at work are bad. In fact, being in a relationship with someone who works in the same industry can be a huge advantage. Working in the masculine industries brings its own challenges that differ from other industries. Often the days are long and tiring, sometimes you work in remote locations away from home and often you're dealing with stressful situations. Having someone who can understand and even relate to what you're going through makes things easier. When you are in a relationship with someone who doesn't understand the challenges of the industry, it can be difficult balancing their expectations with your own. Personally, I have found this tricky, particularly when working on especially demanding projects. Trying to learn how to balance the needs of your loved ones, when all your energy is going towards work can be difficult.

Finding this balance is a constant struggle for me and as such, feeling guilty is a common emotion.

Guilt

It's a theme that has been present in my own career and seems to be pervasive in most commentary about women in the workplace.

Guilt comes from many sources; from never feeling quite good enough, to letting loved ones down, to not giving 100% at work, or 100% to family and even to not taking care of yourself enough. We all have points of guilt, but I think this is especially strong for working women and working mothers.

Now, as a childless working woman, I can only refer to the stories of my peers with children to understand the guilt that working mother's experience. I can only imagine it's another level of guilt. Advanced guilt. However, guilt does not necessarily rest only with the working mums.

I recently met a Human Resource Manager at a networking event who works in the Oil and Gas industry. We were discussing her experiences as a wife who works long hours, with site travel required, and who is married to an investment banker who also has a high-pressure workload. What interested me most from our conversation were her comments about how good it was when her husband worked late so she didn't have to feel guilty for doing the same thing. Her comment resonated with me. How many times have I been thankful when my other half was busy in the evening, or occupied on the weekend, so I could cram in a few extra hours of work or study without feeling like I was neglecting him. I thought this was just my own selfishness (in chasing my goals) and inability to find the elusive "balance", but here was another woman saying the same thing. I wanted to give her a hug! But since we were the only two women in a room full of male managers, I thought it best not.

This got me to wondering, does her husband feel guilty for working late and not being home for her?

Or is this a woman thing?

Whilst the broad research is not conclusive on whether guilt is a male or female emotion, there does tend to be a leaning towards guilt being felt more intensely by women (Etxebarria, Ortiz, Conejero & Pascual, 2009). The tendency for women to experience guilt has often been put down to the belief that women are more focused on interpersonal relationships and hence feel bad when they do something that may disappoint or upset another person.

As Raji, a Health, Safety and Environment Advisor in the construction industry reports, guilt is something she feels "All the time. My friends and family always pressure me into trying to meet up while I'm on R&R but with such a limited amount of time off it's hard to fit in seeing everyone and having a break yourself. I find it hard to stay in regular contact with everyone. By the time you get home from work after a 12-hour shift all you want to do is eat something, have a hot shower and go to bed."

The lifestyle of a FIFO worker can often make balancing relationships very difficult. However, FIFO workers are not the only ones to experience guilt in the industry. Jann, a Senior Industrial Relations Advisor is a large mining organisation, spoke about the difficulty she experienced when coming back to work after 12 months maternity leave. Not only did she feel pangs of guilt for leaving her young child, but she also felt anxious about not understanding what was being discussed in meetings and guilty for not keeping up.

The concept of working mothers' guilt is well documented and discussed. Therefore, I don't wish to repeat it other than to bring your attention to an interesting piece of research which may help alleviate any guilt mothers may feel when returning to work. An early piece of research coming out of the Harvard Business School is finding that working mothers are having a positive effect on gender parity, not only for themselves but also for their children. Of 31,000 people surveyed across 24 developed countries it was found that "Women whose mothers worked outside the home are more likely to have jobs themselves, are more likely to hold supervisory responsibility at those jobs, and earn higher wages than women whose mothers stayed home full time. Men raised by working mothers are more likely to contribute to household chores and spend more time caring for family members" (Nobel, 2015).

Of the 33% of women who admitted to feeling guilty in The BCW survey, interpersonal relationships were only one source of guilt. Other women reported feeling guilty about job performance: "I feel guilty if I don't achieve most things ahead of time" or when "I feel I'm not working hard enough I feel very guilty". Other women report feeling guilty for their life choices: "I gave up a lot of my life - I have no children because I was too busy working away and probably never will". Another woman who has experienced guilt during her life is Li, a Risk Manager in the Construction industry. Li reports "There's a perception my career choice has led me to being a single, childless woman. Maybe that's correct... but it's more likely I just haven't met anyone yet!"

These reports of feeling guilty for matters other than interpersonal relationships are an indication of the type of guilt that can emerge from the changing role definitions women have experienced over the past few decades. The old cliché' of 'having it all" and having choices potentially leaves a lingering thought that we *should* be doing it all because we can. Even though we know having it all is a complete delusion, it is still woven into our psyche and is hard to shake.

These women appear to be pressuring themselves to work hard and be successful, but because they do not have children they are deemed less successful as a woman. I imagine this perception is held within themselves, as is evident from their self-report in the survey, but may also be indicative of the messages they are receiving from family, friends and even society in general.

Personally, I've felt plenty of pressure to have kids, whilst simultaneously being encouraged to chase a career and use the expensive education I spent years completing. Frankly, these conversations get tiresome, especially when I haven't decided which path is for me. Or even if I'm capable of walking the paths simultaneously. Or what it's going to be like to jump off one path onto another, and if I do, will the other path be there when I look for it later. Seriously, it's freaking difficult and nearly all of the women

I speak to around my age (*cough, early 30s), have the same worries.

So have all our choices caused more guilt for women because we now have more categories to feel bad and to "fail" at? Would life be easier if we had less choice? My mum and I have often had this conversation, particularly around her experience of being a working mother in the 1980s in a small country town where it was more acceptable for women to stay home with the kids rather than go to work.

My mum was one of those women who sailed against the cultural norms of her time. Not in a loud, placard waving, dominant way, but rather in her unassuming and doggedly determined way. Before I was born, mum worked at the ANZ bank as a teller. She recounts stories of young male bank tellers starting on higher salaries than the female tellers who had been employed for years. Where she could only wear skirts and dresses to work as women were not allowed to wear pants. And where she could not take a credit card out in her own name, even though she was a bank employee, as only men could apply for credit cards (with the woman being the secondary signature). A few months before my birth, Mum took "maternity leave" from the bank (which was really just unpaid leave). Yet rather than enjoying her time off, she got bored and wanted to make some extra money to help the family. Mum picked up a few shifts a week at a local Armaguard branch counting money. She had planned on doing this for as long as she could, but I had other plans and decided to pop into the world a month early (sorry mum!).

After my birth, Mum returned to part-time work when I was 6 weeks old. She says her decision was not an easy one, but that it came down to a number of factors: Firstly, she enjoyed working and the feelings that it gave to her and her self-esteem; Secondly, she didn't think it was fair that Dad was out working whilst she was at home; and thirdly, the additional income was beneficial to our young family. At the time though, Mum says she worried every single day whether she was doing the right thing by me. She worried that by working, she would be damaging me in some way and that she would be considered a bad mother for leaving me with carers. When I asked her whether Dad would have had the same worries, she said "No. Back in those days it was presumed the male would work, because usually he would be the one making more money". I also would imagine that since it was a social norm for the man to work, Dad would not have had the same child related worries as Mum did since child rearing was still very much a female job. Instead, Dad's worries focused more around providing financial security to his family.

Throughout this section it has become apparent that worries are tied to guilt. Perhaps, we could go so far as to say that worrying is the root of guilt. If we didn't worry about what others thought, whether we were disappointing or letting people down, or what unknowns may be lurking in the future, then maybe we wouldn't hold so much guilt for our choices in the present?

Yet worrying, is not good for your health. Worrying triggers the stress hormones which if experienced over a prolonged period can lead to physical reactions including headaches, nausea, disrupted sleep, heart irregularities and a suppressed immune system. These are all things we could definitely do without.

Being mindful of when and where you feel guilt is the first step to dealing with this emotion. Then, rather than stuff it back into your unconscious mind, you need to spend time exploring it. This can be the hardest part, particularly when guilt is such an uncomfortable emotion to be exploring. It can often be useful to understand that guilt stems from not living up to your own expectations (which are often influenced by, but are external to, the expectations of others) and from the judgement you place on yourself for not meeting your ideals. By recognising that we are all perfectly imperfect, and we are all trying to figure out our lives (irrespective of how old we are) we can begin to be a little kinder to ourselves. If you can influence the reason for feeling guilty, and you wish to change something, then go ahead. But if you feel you can't change what is causing your guilt then I would suggest it's time to question how useful holding on to that guilt really is. What does it give you other than that gnawing feeling of self-deprecation and disappointment? Perhaps it's time we were all a little kinder to ourselves.

Women Supporting Women

Speaking of being kinder to ourselves, I think we also need to discuss being kinder to one another. As we near the end of this book I felt it fitting to turn our attention towards the relationships amongst women in the masculine industries. Since we're the minority, I'm always drawn to other women who work in masculine environments and who occupy jobs which are not traditionally occupied by women. I want to know their stories, their challenges and what they've done to overcome them. It's been this curiosity that has led me to share this book with you all.

Throughout the years I've come across women who want to share their stories and others who don't want anything to do with the "women in (insert industry)" movement. The first group are the ones who join the committees, promote diversity (not just gender diversity) and speak up about inequality when they see it. The latter group tends to get on with their role, without considering gender has anything to do with the workplace and without joining the movement for greater gender equality.

Whilst I admire the women in the latter group for their focus on getting in and doing their jobs, it bothers me they turn their back on such a glaring and obvious inequality. Frankly, I find it a little bit selfish. Just because you haven't experienced certain challenges doesn't mean they don't exist for others. It's like ignoring racism because you haven't experienced it. Or ignoring poverty and famine because you've got plenty to eat.

The statistics are clear; the overwhelming majority of women are not treated equally to men, even though there are a few women reaching great career heights. Not every woman has the same experiences, circumstances and traits that will enable her to follow a similar path. The women who have made it without encountering any gender-related challenges have, quite simply, been lucky. Lucky to have had particular experiences, lucky to have had certain role models or influences throughout their life, lucky to have innate or developed skills that have enabled them to succeed. This luck in no way detracts from their hard work and skills, nor does it denigrate or devalue their achievements. Rather, it signifies that certain factors have been involved in this successful woman's life that other women have not had access to, or simply didn't know about. Therefore, we need to help other women access these success factors to enable more women to achieve their dreams and reach their full potential.

As a woman, I believe we have a bond and even an obligation to other women to share these lessons. To help out our fellow ladies and to support them to achieve what they want. I'm going to go so far as to say women should support women for no other reason than the fact we're all women. There are enough challenges in the world for women and girls, we should not be adding to them within our gender. Of course, I would ultimately like to see this concept of helping one another be expanded to all humans, but we're a long way from this being a reality, so let's focus on a smaller subset.

The concept of women supporting women tends to get challenged by the idea that women are inherently competitive with one another or that they don't really like one another. I've seen this message get played out on mine sites where women "have to be" separated on different crews because of their fighting. I'm also sure most women would have encountered another female at some point in their life who was deliberately cold, mean or downright nasty to them for no apparent reason.

What I have learnt is that these types of women (and men for that matter) tend to act this way because of their own insecurities, anxieties and often jealousies. These women are usually not inherently bad people; rather, they are being influenced by social messages (family, media, workplaces) that constantly tell them they're not good enough. To try to make themselves feel better, they seek out other people to put down so they can feel better about who they are. Yet rather than this actually making them feel better, they may feel elements of remorse, which makes them dislike themselves even further, and leads them to lash out against others all over again. It's a twisted cycle that keeps on repeating.

So as women in the masculine industries we need to be careful not to get caught up in comparing ourselves against our female colleagues. This can be tricky, especially when there are so many awards and recognitions for women working in non-traditional industries that unintentionally it could be causing comparison and competition between women. It's also difficult when there is a sense of pride of being the only woman on site (or one of a few). When I asked two young female engineers whether they would be happy with more women in their workplace, they were slow to answer. They ultimately said yes, it would even things up, make them feel more accepted and would change some of the dominant male behaviour – particularly the behaviour displayed by the older male site supervisors they dealt with regularly. However, their answer didn't satisfy me as I felt there was something else in their mind. I arranged to have dinner with one of the girls, and after a couple of wines I asked her the question again, "would you like to work with more women on site?". This time, she leant forward and quietly admitted, "you know what, I like being the girl, it's special. You feel proud to tell people you work in mining and to see their shock". Finally, she'd told the truth.

This sense of pride or being "special" is something I can relate to. When you tell people that you work in a masculine industry, most people tend to be somewhat shocked, and then interested. I had an electrician come to our house one day to fix some wiring. He started off being incredibly condescending and talking down to me about the general manliness of fixing stuff. This guy seemed to have a stereotype in mind that I would know nothing about handiwork and was cold and dismissive of my questions. That was until I managed to weave in my work in trade environments and geeze, didn't that change his tune. Next thing you know he was talking to me about what he was doing with the wiring, what he thought was wrong with it, and how he was going to fix it. My partner overheard this entire conversation (he was upstairs working in his office as maintenance does not really float his boat) and thought the conversation was quite hilarious; from my obvious indignation at being dismissed to the man's complete change of tune after hearing where I worked.

I know I personally get a kick out of telling people I work in mining and construction and to see them look impressed. It does make you feel special and different. Therefore, I can understand if there are women already in the industry who, deep down on some level, feel resentful if more women enter the industry and devalue the sense of pride they feel for being one of the "only girls" on site. It's understandable, especially if you place a lot of weight on that aspect defining who you are.

However, if we are truly going to work together, to shift an industry culture that could do with a bit more balance, we need to change our perspectives as women. To the women who are already working in the industries, you are the ones leading the way. You have done, and in many cases, are still doing, the hard yards to break stereotypes and change perceptions about women in industry. Nothing will change this. Therefore, rather than take pride in being "a" woman in a masculine industry, why not be proud of being "one of the first" women in the industries who are now paving the way for other women. Be the mentor, the role model, the advocate for others who are entering and beginning to find their feet in an industry that truly does have different rules for women compared to men.

This is the role I hope you all take. And I hope you find immense value, personal pride and an overarching sense of being part of something bigger than yourself.

You are the pioneers, be proud of your achievements, but make sure you lay the foundations for the next generation of women to come.

Behaviours & Relationships

(What Girl Are You? Sex & Relationships, Guilt, Women
Supporting Women)

Start...

Stop...

Continue...

Conclusion

"Whatever women do they must do twice as well as men to be thought half as good. Luckily, this is not difficult."
– Charlotte Whitton

Being a woman is not an easy job.

Being a woman in a masculine industry is an even harder job.

You must navigate the challenges, the stereotypes, the biases and the inequality all before you can even get on with what you are being paid to do in your role.

It has been my wish throughout this book to help women understand and navigate the unspoken rules of the game of being a woman in a masculine industry. By exploring the culture of the industry and sharing the stories of women who have come before us we can learn from their experiences and give ourselves a head start to achieving success. It is hoped that through this book you can begin to analyse your own behaviour and actions at work, decide whether they're giving you the outcome you need and make a strategic choice about how you want to move forward. What will you stop doing, what will you start doing and what will you continue to do?

I also encourage you to debate the content in this book. It should cause discussion and it should be challenged. After all, the content contained is only a small subset of the experiences of the approximately 50,000 women who work across the masculine industries of Australia. However, the stories I have heard and the experiences I've encountered myself are enough to tell me that something is not right in our masculine industries. That our cultures need to change to make these workplaces not only more accepting and inclusive of women, but also to other people who aren't white, heterosexual males. For too long our organisations have been favourably biased towards this subset of humans. And whilst they have done a pretty good job in running the show, it's time to be even better. In fact, we must be even better. If Australia wants to compete on the global stage, if we want to set up our country for future prosperity and growth, we need to look beyond our existing norms. It's time to be diverse in our thinking, to challenge the status quo and do things differently. Otherwise, we'll be left behind, and that would be a crying shame for a country that has achieved so much in only a couple of hundred years.

The other intention of this book is to connect women together. Many resource, construction and engineering projects are located in remote areas. This means many women live and work in locations where populations are small, and there are less people who you can share similarities with. It's not uncommon to be one of only a few women on a site, and it can be a very isolating feeling when there's no one to talk honestly with about how you feel and the challenges you're experiencing. The Blue Collared Woman social media accounts and website were developed to help women in these locations to connect with others in similar experiences. This book has been written for women to realise they are not alone in what they're experiencing.

Finding this commonality and building relationships with women across the industry is important. We are all in this together. We are all responsible for supporting other women, helping other women and encouraging other women to achieve. It doesn't matter if we do things differently or we have a different opinion – this difference is our strength. It means we cannot be defined, we cannot be put in a box or stereotyped. Together we are stronger. Together we can help each other succeed. We can pull other women up with us as we rise and we can make room for her at the table. We owe this to the women who have forged the path before us, and we owe it to our daughters and granddaughters to come. We all share an unshakable bond that can never be destroyed.

We are all women.

And we are powerful.

References

Agthe, M., Spörrle. M. & Maner, J. K. (2011). Does Being Attractive Always Help? Positive and Negative Effects of Attractiveness on Social Decision Making, *Personality and Social Psychology Bulletin, 37*(8), 1042-1054.

Australian Broadcasting Commission. *Mental health nursing is 'most dangerous profession' in Victoria, new research finds.* (2014). Retrieved, March 15, 2015, from http://www.abc.net.au/news/2014-08-08/mental-health-nursing-the-27most-dangerous-profession27-in-vi/5657464.

Australian Bureau of Statistics. (2004). *Suicides: Recent Trends, Australia 1993-2003.* Retrieved February 27, 2015, from http://andrewleigh.org/pdf/ABS_suicide_rates_Australia.pdf.

Australian Bureau of Statistics. (2012). *Causes of Death, Australia.* Retrieved February 27, 2015, from http://www.abs.gov.au/ausstats/abs@.nsf/Lookup/by%20Subject/3303.0~2012~Main%20Features~Contents~1.

Australian Bureau of Statistics. (2015). *Average Weekly Earnings, Australia, Nov 2014.* Retrieved March 27, 2015, from http://www.abs.gov.au/ausstats/abs@.nsf/mf/6302.0.

Australian Government Department of Employment. (2014). *Industry Outlook: Mining.* Retrieved January 01, 2016, from https://cica.org.au/wp-content/uploads/2014-Mining-Industry-Employment-Outlook1.pdf.

Australian Government Department of Health and Ageing. (2013). *National Mental Health Report: Tracking progress of mental health reform in Australia, 1993-2011.* Retrieved February 27, 2015, from https://www.health.gov.au/internet/main/publishing.nsf/content/B090F03865A7FAB9CA257C1B0079E198/$File/rep13.pdf.

Australian Human Rights Commission. (2012). *Working Without Fear: Results of the Sexual Harassment National Telephone Survey.* Retrieved March 30, 2015, from https://www.humanrights.gov.au/sites/default/files/content/sexualharassment/survey/SHSR_2012%20Web%20Version%20Final.pdf.

Babcock, L. & Laschever, S. (2003). *Women Don't Ask: Negotiation and the Gender Divide.* Princeton University Press.

Barsh, J. & Yee, L. (2011). Unlocking the full potential of women in the US economy. *McKinsey & Company.* Retrieved June 08, 2015, from http://www.mckinsey.com/client_service/organization/latest_thinking/unlocking_the_full_potential

Barta, T., Kleiner, M. & Neumann, T. (2012). Is there a payoff from top team diversity? *McKinsey Quarterly*. Retrieved June 08, 2015 from http://www.mckinsey.com/business-functions/organization/our-insights/is-there-a-payoff-from-top-team-diversity.

Baruch, Y. & Jenkins, S. (2007). Swearing at work and permissive leadership culture: When anti-social becomes social and incivility is acceptable. Leadership & Organization Development Journal, 28(6), pp.492 – 507.Beyer, S. (1990). Gender Differences in the Accuracy of Self-Evaluations of Performance. *Journal of Personality and Social Psychology,* 59(5), 960–970.

Brizendine, L., (2010). *The Male Brain*. London, Transworld Publishers.

Carney, D. R., Hall, J. A. & Smith LBeau, L. (2005). Beliefs About the Nonverbal Expression of Social Power. *Journal of Nonverbal Behaviour, 29*(2), 105-123.

Cha. Y. & Weeden, K. A. (2014). Overwork and the Slow Convergence in the Gender Gap in Wages. *American Sociological Review*, 1-28.

Chaplin, J.B., Phillips, J.B., Brown, J. D., Clanton, N. R. & Stein, J. L. (2000). Handshaking, Gender, Personality and First Impressions. *Journal of Personality and Social Psychology, 79*(1), 110-117.

Cole, D. A., Martin, J. M., Peeke, L. A., Seroczynski, A. D. & Fier, J. (1999). Children's Over- and Underestimation of Academic Competence: A Longitudinal Study of Gender Differences, Depression and Anxiety. *Child Development*, *70*(2), 459-473.

Commonwealth of Australia (2010). Taking Preventative Action – A Response to Australia: The Healthiest Country by 2020: The Report of the National Preventative Health Taskforce. Retrieved February 27, 2015, from http://www.google.com.au/url?sa=t&rct=j&q=&esrc=s&source=web&cd=1&ve d=0ahUKEwiu_sWl4bfMAhWi3aYKHVQPBO8QFggbMAA&url=http%3A%2 F%2Fwww.preventativehealth.org.au%2Finternet%2Fpreventativehealth%2Fpu blishing.nsf%2FContent%2F6B7B17659424FBE5CA25772000095458%2F%24 File%2Ftpa.pdf&usg=AFQjCNHh-RPbVllsE9Irsw2-q-JzIxaKJw&bvm=bv.121070826,d.dGY

Contreras, J. M., Banaji, M. R. & Mitchel, J. P. (2014). Multivoxel Patterns in Fusiform Face Area Differentiate Faces by Sex and Race. *PLoS ONE 8*(7). Retrieved March, 09, 2015 from http://journals.plos.org/plosone/article?id=10.1371/journal.pone.0069684#abstra ct0

Daubman, K. A. and Sigall, H. (1997). Gender differences in perceptions of how others are affected by self-disclosure of achievement. *Sex Roles, 37*(1-2), 73-89.

Dolcos, S., Sung, K., Argo, J. J., Flor-Henry, S., & Dolcos, F. (2012). The Power of a Handshake: Neural Correlates of Evaluative Judgments in Observed Social Interactions. *Journal of Cognitive Neuroscience, 24*(12), 2292-2305.

249

Driskell, J. E., Copper, C. & Moran, A. (1994). Does Mental Practice Enhance Performance? *Journal of Applied Psychology*, *79*(4),481-492.

Duke University. (2010). Some males react to competition like bonobos, others like chimpanzees. *ScienceDaily*. Retrieved February 20, 2015 from www.sciencedaily.com/releases/2010/06/100628152637.htm.

Erol, R. Y. & Orth, U. (2011). Self-Esteem Development from Age 14 to 30 years: A Longitudinal Study. *Journal of Personality and Social Psychology, 101*(3), 607-619.

Etcoff, N.L., Stock, S, Haley. L. E., Vickery, S.A. & House, D. M. (2011). *Cosmetics as a Feature of the Extended Human Phenotype: Modulation of the Perception of Biologically Important Facial Signals.* PLoS ONE 6(10). Retrieved February 29, 2015, from http://journals.plos.org/plosone/article/asset?id=10.1371%2Fjournal.pone.00256 56.PDF.

Etxebarria, I., Ortiz, M. H., Conejero, S. & Pascual, A. (2009). Intensity of Habitual Guilt in Men and Women: Differences in Interpersonal Sensitivity and the Tendency towards Anxious-Aggressive Guilt. *The Spanish Journal of Psychology, 12*(2), 540-554.

European Parliament (2010). *The Policy on gender equality in Iceland. Women's Rights and Gender Equality.* Retrieved May 12, 2015, from http://www.europarl.europa.eu/document/activities/cont/201107/20110725ATT2 4624/20110725ATT24624EN.pdf.

Forret, M. L. & Dougherty, T. W. (2004). Networking behaviours and career outcomes: Differences for men and women? *Journal of Organizational Behaviour, 25*, 419-437.

Frankel, L. P. (2010). *Nice Girls Don't Get the Corner Office: 101 Unconscious Mistakes Women Make That Sabotage Their Careers.* New York, Business Plus.

Gneezy, U., Niederle, M. & Rustichini, A. (2003). Performance in Competitive Environments: Gender Differences. *Quarterly Journal of Economics, 118*(3), 1049–1074.

Heilman, M.E., Wallen, A. S., Fuchs, D. & Tamkins, M. M. (2004). Penalties for Success: Reactions to Women Who Succeed at Male Gender-Typed Tasks. *Journal of Applied Psychology, 89*(3), 416-427.

Huntsdale, J. (2014). *Australia's drinking problem the focus of Australian Medical Association summit in Canberra.* Retrieved March 22, 2015, from http://www.abc.net.au/news/2014-10-28/ama-alcohol-summit/5847186.

Ibarra, H., Carter, N. M. & Silva, C. (2010). Why Men Still Get More Promotions Than Women. *Harvard Business Review*. Retrieved October 11, 2015, from https://hbr.org/2010/09/why-men-still-get-more-promotions-than-women#.

Isaac, A. R. (1992). Mental Practice- Does it Work in the Field? *The Sport Psychologist, 6*, 192-198.

Johnson, S.K., Podratz, K. E., Dipboye, R. L. & Gibbons, E. (2010). Physical Attractiveness Biases in Ratings of Employment Suitability: Tracking Down the "Beauty is Beastly" Effect. *The Journal of Social Psychology, 150*(3), 301-318.

Kehinde, A. J., Ogugu, S. E., James, B. I., Paul, D. K., Racheal, A. M. et al. (2012). Tears Production: Implication for Health Enhancement. *Open Access Scientific Reports, 1(*10), 2-8.

Lakoff, R. (1973). Language and Woman's Place. *Language in Society,* 2(1), 45-80.

Laplonge, D. (2014). So you think you're tough? Getting serious about gender in mining. Sydney, Factive.

Legislative Assembly, Parliament of Western Australia (2015). The impact of FIFO work practices on mental health: Final Report. Retrieved January 03, 2016, from http://www.parliament.wa.gov.au/Parliament/commit.nsf/(Report+Lookup+by+Com+ID)/2E970A7A4934026448257E67002BF9D1/$file/20150617%20-%20Final%20Report%20w%20signature%20for%20website.pdf.

Marks, M. & Harold, C (2011). Who asks and who receives in Salary negotiation. *Journal of Organisational Behaviour, 32*, 371-394.

Mason, M. F., Lee, A. J., Wiley, E. A. & Ames, D. R. (2013). Precise offers are potent anchors: Conciliatory counteroffers and attributions of knowledge in negotiations, *Journal of Experimental Social Psychology*, 49(4), 759-763.

Mehdizadeh, L. Sturrock, A. Myers, G., Khatib, Y. Dacre, J. (2014). How well do doctors think they perform on the General Medical Council's Tests of Competence pilot examinations? A cross-sectional study. *BMJ Open.* Retrieved October 15, 2015, from http://bmjopen.bmj.com/content/4/2/e004131.full.pdf+html.

Ministerial Council on Drug Strategy. (2006). National Alcohol Strategy 2006-2009, Commonwealth of Australia May 2006. Retrieved March 22, 2015, from http://www.alcohol.gov.au/internet/alcohol/publishing.nsf/Content/nas-06-09

Niederle, M. and Vesterlund, L. (2011). Gender and Competition. *Annual Review of Economics, 3,* 601-630.

Nobel, C. (2015). Children Benefit From Having a Working Mom, *Harvard Business School.* Retrieved October 25, 2015 from http://www.hbs.edu/news/articles/Pages/mcginn-working-mom.aspx

Preston, S. D., Buchanan, T. W., Stansfield, R. B., & Bechara, A. (2007). Effects of anticipatory stress on decision making in a gambling task. *Behavioral Neuroscience, 121,* 257–263.

Robinson, D. T. & Smith-Lovin, L. (2001). Getting a Laugh: Gender, Status and Humour in Task Discussions. *Social Forces, 80*(1): 123-158

Roche, A. M., Fischer, J., Pidd, Ken., Lee, N., Battams, S. & Nicholas, R. (2012). Workplace mental illness and substance use disorders in male-dominated industries: A Systematic Literature Review. *National Centre for Education and Training on Addiction (NCETA)*, December.

Safe Work Australia (2015). Worker Fatalities, March 2015. Retrieved March 24, 2015, from http://www.safeworkaustralia.gov.au/sites/swa/statistics/work-related-fatalities/pages/worker-fatalities.

Sainz, M. & Eccles, J. (2012). Self-concept of computer and math ability: Gender implications across time and within ICT studies. *Journal of Vocational Behaviour, 80, 486 – 499.*

Smith, J. (2013). *10 Reasons Why Humor Is A Key To Success At Work.* Retrieved October 25, 2015, from http://www.forbes.com/sites/jacquelynsmith/2013/05/03/10-reasons-why-humor-is-a-key-to-success-at-work/2/.

Snyder, K. (2014). *The abrasiveness trap: High-achieving men and women are described differently in reviews.* Retrieved October 14, 2015, from http://fortune.com/2014/08/26/performance-review-gender-bias/.

Starcke,K., Polzer, C., Wolf, O.T., & Brand, M. (2011). Does stress alter everyday moral decision-making? *Psychoneuroendocrinology, 36*, 210.

Stephens, R., Atkins, J. & Kingston, A. (2009). Swearing as a response to pain. *Neuroreport, 20*(12), 1056-1060.

Stets, J. E. & Burke, P. J. (2000). Femininity/Masculinity. In E. F. Borgatta & R. J. V. Montgomery (Eds.), *Encyclopedia of Sociology.* New York: Macmillan.

Vingerhoets, A. J. J. M., Cornelius, R. R., Van Heck, G. L. & Becht, M. C. (2000). Adult Crying: A model and review of the literature. *Review of General Psychology, 4*(4), 354-377.

Vingerhoets A. (2013). *Why Only Humans Weep: Unravelling the Mysteries of Tears.* Oxford: Oxford University Press.

Wessel, J.L., Hagiwara, N., Ryan, A.M. & Kermond, C. M. (2015). Should Women Applicants "Man Up" for Traditionally Masculine Fields? Effectiveness of Two Verbal Identity Management Strategies. *Psychology of Women Quarterly, 39*(2), 243-255.

Wolff, H.-G. & Moser, K (2009). Effects of networking on career success: a longitudinal study. *Journal of Applied Psychology, 94*(1), 196-206.

Workplace Gender Equality Agency. (2015). *Gender composition of the workforce: by industry.* Retrieved December 31, 2015, from https://www.wgea.gov.au/sites/default/files/Gender-composition-of-the-workforce-by-industry.pdf.

Workplace Gender Equality Agency (2015), *Gender pay gap statistics.* Retrieved 01 January, 2016, https://www.wgea.gov.au/sites/default/files/Gender_Pay_Gap_Factsheet.pdf

World Economic Forum (2014). *Global Gender Gap Report*. Retrieved from
http://www3.weforum.org/docs/GGGR14/GGGR_CompleteReport_2014.pdf.

CPSIA information can be obtained
at www.ICGtesting.com
Printed in the USA
BVHW081855050219
539515BV00002B/165/P